J ust then the front door opened. T. J.'s hands dropped to his sides, and he stepped back. In the same instant, Gwen burst away from him and dashed for the front door, practically tumbling into the arms of another strange man who had just stepped into the office.

But at least this man looked respectable. He had on a dark suit and tie and looked as surprised as she was frightened. She looked up at him with pleading eyes, as if begging him to help her.

"What's going on here?" he asked, quickly looking over to where T. J. was still sheepishly standing behind the reception desk.

"I was just leaving," said T. J. as he brushed past the two of them and shot out the door.

Gwen felt her knees turn to jelly, and she collapsed on the couch in the waiting room. "Thank God you came in when you did!"

A PALISADES CONTEMPORARY ROMANCE

SHADES OF LIGHT

Melody Carlson

PALISADES

SHADES OF LIGHT
published by Palisades
a division of Multnomah Publishers, Inc.

© 1998 by Melody Carlson
International Standard Book Number: 1-57673-283-5

Cover illustration by Paul Bachem/Artworks, Inc.
Design by Brenda McGee

Scripture quotations are from:
The Holy Bible, New King James Version
© 1984 by Thomas Nelson, Inc.

Palisades is a trademark of Multnomah Publishers, Inc.,
and is registered in the U.S. Patent and Trademark Office.

Printed in the United States of America

For information:
MULTNOMAH PUBLISHERS, INC.
POST OFFICE BOX 1720
SISTERS, OREGON 97759

Library of Congress Cataloging-in-Publication Data:
Carlson, Melody.
Shades of light / by Melody Carlson.
        p. cm.
ISBN 1-57673-283-5 (alk. paper)
I. Title
PS3553.A73257S53 1998
813'.54—dc21   98–12014
                                          CIP
98 99 00 01 02 03 04 — 10 9 8 7 6 5 4 3 2 1

With love and appreciation to my publishing friends:
Jennifer Brooks, Linda Bennett, and Sue Rodine

Every good gift and every perfect gift is from above,
and comes down from the Father of lights,
with whom there is no variation or shadow of turning.

JAMES 1:17

"Gwen, I think it's about time you began to have a life," Candice said breezily as she moved across the patio refilling the glasses of the many guests. Gwen glanced around self-consciously, then forced a laugh. It was so like Candice Mallard to launch a campaign to reinvent Gwen's life in the company of strangers.

"I have a life, Candice," Gwen said in an apologetic tone. She stood, picked up an empty appetizer plate, and began to move toward the kitchen. "And if you want to have a dinner, I better go and check on the lamb." She hoped her exasperation didn't show in her voice.

Candice laughed. "Yes, my dear, go check on the lovely lamb. One would think that I had invited you here tonight just so you could help out in the kitchen."

Gwen smiled. "You mean you didn't?"

Now it was Candice who looked slightly uncomfortable, and for that Gwen was sorry. Sorry for her words, but even more sorry that she was probably right. She went into Candice's efficient-looking kitchen and checked the oversized convection oven. It was a dream kitchen, but mostly a show-place because Candice rarely cooked. Since she occasionally brought her clients here to discuss elements of kitchen design, she had used her kitchen as a tax write-off.

The lamb was just fine and probably wouldn't be ready for another thirty minutes. Gwen heard footsteps coming her way and knew it would be Candice. Not quite ready for the rest of their conversation, Gwen slipped into the back bathroom. She turned on the faucet and looked blankly into the mirror.

Was Candice right? Did Gwen really have no life? Gwen's brown eyes stared back at her, but they seemed unfamiliar—dull and sad. People used to say that she had fire in her eyes. It was probably only due to the flecks of gold around the irises, but she used to believe it was because she had a passion for life—a fire burning inside. But for the last two years that passion had been dormant. And now she wondered if she would ever get it back. She pushed a dark brown curl behind her ear and examined her face more closely. The remnant of a summer tan almost obliterated the sprinkling of freckles across her nose, but at least there were no signs of wrinkles yet.

"Gwen," Candice called as she knocked at the door. "I know you're in there. Are you okay? I'm sorry I said that. You know how I am. Gary says words just shoot out my mouth before they ever pass through my brain."

Gwen blew her nose and opened the door. "It's okay, Candice. I'm sorry, too. It's just that this is—you know—a difficult time."

Candice wrapped her arms around Gwen. "I know, honey. That's why I asked you over tonight. I figured that with Aubrey just going off to college, you're probably suffering a case of empty-nest syndrome."

Gwen bristled at the label. "I wouldn't call it that, Candice. It's more than that. I mean, it's barely been two years since I lost David, and—"

"And, and—" Candice threw her hands in the air. "I don't want to hear another word, Gwen. I invited you here tonight to have some fun and meet some people. You're too young to give up on life. Come on back out. You've hardly met anyone. You know, Gary has a friend he wants you to meet. He's an attorney, too. New in town. Recently divorced."

"Just what I need," said Gwen.

"Oh, don't be such a wet blanket."

Gwen obediently followed Candice back out to the patio and settled into a wrought-iron chair. Already Candice was making her rounds again. She had always been socially adept. Even in grade school, it was Candice who made things happen. As a child, Gwen had been intimidated by Candice's outspoken confidence. Even when they became better friends in high school, Gwen had always maintained a safe distance. They had never been best friends. Gwen had never trusted Candice that much.

Like the rest of her house, Candice's patio was perfection. With terra-cotta tile and massive fern- and flower-filled pots, heavy wrought-iron furniture, and a fountain splashing pleasantly in the corner, it could have been Rome. It was lovely, but with the vine-covered patio roof, it was a little on the dark side for Gwen's taste.

Gwen liked light. She never seemed to get enough of it. Candice on the other hand seemed to thrive on darkness. She said it was cozy. She liked rich colors, heavy ornate drapes, and dark massive furnishings. Apparently her clients did, too, because her interior design business seemed to be thriving.

"Gwen, come on over here," called Candice. "I want you to meet Mary and Ray Powers. They just bought the Randall estate last year. Ray's in investments, and Mary's a real-estate agent." She turned to the couple. "And Gwen Sullivan is an old friend of mine. She lives just down the street. As you've probably heard, she's also an excellent cook, and she's overseeing the main dish for dinner tonight."

"Nice to meet you, Gwen," said the pretty blond woman. "Candice is redecorating our home. And doing a fantastic job, I might add."

"And for what she charges, it had better be spectacular," said the man with a lopsided grin that looked as if he was partly serious.

Candice playfully punched him in the arm. "From what I hear, you can afford it, Ray. Mary told me you just made a killing last week."

Ray grimaced. "A killing one day, killed the next. Don't let one good week give you any grandiose ideas, Candice. I don't want to come home to find a Picasso hanging in my bathroom."

Candice tilted her head to one side. "No, Ray, I was thinking more along the lines of Renoir. You know how Mary goes for the more romantic style." Candice smiled slyly and began to move to the other end of the patio, chatting and joking as she went.

Mary laughed and then quickly changed the subject. "And what do you do, Gwen?"

Gwen took in a deep breath. *What did she do?* "Well, I've mostly been a homemaker." She paused. "Of course, I've always been involved in community things and whatnot. The garden club and school functions. But now with my daughter going off to college—"

"No way," interrupted Ray. "You can't possibly have a daughter old enough for college."

Gwen nodded. "It's true. We started our family earlier than people do nowadays."

"You must have been in preschool." Ray chuckled.

"Thanks," said Gwen. "Actually it's nice having a grown daughter. She's been a very good friend."

"And what does your husband do?" asked Ray. His wife elbowed him. "I'm sorry, Gwen. I get in trouble for that all the time. I know I shouldn't presume that you are married." Ray reminded her of a five-year-old repeating an apology that he'd been forced to give more than once.

"Actually, my husband was killed in a car wreck almost two years ago."

"I'm so sorry," Mary said with true empathy. She gently squeezed Gwen's arm.

"It was hard at first, but at least Aubrey and I had each other. She is a lot like her dad. In fact, she even got a basketball scholarship at the same college my husband played for over twenty years ago."

"She must be pretty good," said Ray. "I didn't think they gave out too many basketball scholarships to women."

Gwen smiled. "She led her high-school team to state three years in a row."

"Impressive," said Ray. "Come to think of it, I remember reading about it in the paper."

"So, now that your daughter is off to college," said Mary, "do you have any career interests that you plan to pursue?"

Gwen thought for a moment. "Oh, I suppose I have some old dreams. But they're probably not very realistic." She glanced over at Candice. "I don't have any formal training like Candice, but I've always enjoyed interior decor. I used to work in my husband's furniture store—for customers, you know. But I really enjoyed it, and some people thought I had a knack for decorating. It was fun."

"No kidding?" said Mary. "You should be working with Candice."

"Oh, I don't think so—" began Gwen.

"Seriously," said Mary. "Candice told me just last week that she was shorthanded and needed to hire someone. With your daughter going off to college and all, it would be a nice change of pace for you."

"Oh, I don't think that Candice—" But once again Gwen was cut off.

"It would be perfect!" exclaimed Mary triumphantly. Ray was nodding, too.

"Candice," called Ray. "Come back here. We have just come up with a splendid idea for you."

Gwen looked on in horror as Ray and Mary proceeded to tell Candice that they had found the answer to all her problems. "And now you have no excuse for not finishing up our house in time for Thanksgiving," proclaimed Ray.

"And may I inquire as to who this wonder woman might be?" Candice asked with an audible edge to her voice. Gwen couldn't bear to look up. For the second time she wished she hadn't come tonight.

"Why she's been sitting right under your nose," Mary said as she patted Gwen's knee. "Your friend Gwen has an interest in interior decorating. And with her daughter going off to college, I'd say the timing is just perfect."

"And," Ray said in an almost accusatory tone, "haven't you been saying that you were shorthanded?"

Candice looked at Gwen with raised brows. "I seriously doubt that Gwen would want to work for me."

Mary looked at Gwen. "I don't know why not. What do you think, Gwen?"

Gwen forced a laugh. "I don't think that Candice would really be interested in hiring me," she said uncomfortably. If only this conversation could end. "I wonder if I should go check on the lamb, Candice?"

"That sounds like a good idea," said Candice stiffly.

Gwen could still hear Mary and Ray continue to prod Candice about their new idea as she went into the house. The pair of them reminded her of overzealous matchmakers—good intentions but slightly obsessed.

She checked the lamb again and gave it a final basting. It looked like it would be done soon. Perhaps it would be safer to wait in the kitchen until Candice forgot about the Powers's suggestion. She sat down at the little desk that Candice had neatly designed into a corner of the kitchen and absently began to flip through the interior design magazine lying there. She used to study these magazines with real interest. But she hadn't picked one up since David's death. Shortly after his funeral she had been cashed out of David's portion of the family furniture business and politely told that her skills were no longer needed in the store. It had hurt at the time, but there had been so much other pain that she hadn't really noticed until it was too late. By then David's brother's wife had taken over that part of the business. But it wasn't long before several former customers crossed Gwen's path and hinted that the new decorator was not nearly as talented as Gwen. It seemed all Shawna wanted to do was sweet pastels with flowers and frills. And while it was reassuring to Gwen to know that her skills were missed, it was too late to do anything about it as far as the furniture store went.

"So, here is my little kitchen slave," said Candice.

"It seemed like a safe haven." Gwen stood and faced Candice. "I'm really sorry about the Powers. Believe me, I had no idea they were going to pull something like that. Please, don't give it another thought, Candice."

"Now, don't be so hasty, Gwen. I must admit that it took me by surprise. It's true, I had been thinking about hiring someone. But I did want someone with more experience."

"What kind of experience?" asked Gwen, with an unexpected feeling of hopefulness. "You do remember that I used to run the interior design department at Sullivan's."

Candice frowned. "No offense intended, Gwen, but Sullivan's Fine Furnishings is pretty small potatoes compared to the clientele I deal with. Besides, I need someone with more office skills."

"Maybe I could learn those things, Candice. At least I have a pretty good understanding of decor. I know how to measure for window coverings, flooring, and whatever, and I have excellent furniture knowledge—"

"This isn't an interview, Gwen."

"I'm sorry." Gwen went over to check on the lamb again, keeping her back to Candice. She knew that the idea of working for Candice was probably insane. The smartest thing would be to drop the idea right now.

"It's not that I wouldn't *like* to give you a job, Gwen."

Gwen carefully removed the steaming lamb from the oven. It looked perfect. "I better check the mint sauce," she said as she put the pot holders away.

"Oh, what the heck," said Candice. "Why don't you give it a try?"

"What?" Gwen asked, turning to look at Candice.

"Why don't you come in on Monday? We can give it a shot. And if it doesn't work out after a few weeks, we'll still be friends, okay?"

"Oh, I don't know. I mean this is so unexpected. It could be a big mistake, Candice. And I haven't even had time to give it any serious thought."

"What's there to think about? It's a job. And you probably need something to keep you busy. And I don't know how good David's insurance was, but you have a kid in college, and that can't be cheap."

Gwen thought about that. Finances were not a problem,

but she knew that wouldn't always be the case. "Well, if you really think you'd want me, I could give it a try. I am a hard worker."

Candice nodded. "I know you are, honey. I just hope this is the right thing for both of us. Now, let's let Tammy finish up in here. Besides you still haven't met Willis Newman."

"The divorced lawyer?"

"Let's just think of him as a single attorney, dear," Candice said with a smirk. "It sounds more flattering, don't you think?"

"Whatever you say, boss." Gwen wiped off her hands and followed Candice back out to where the guests were beginning to drift into the spacious house.

"I can feel autumn in the air," said Candice brightly. "Don't you just love this time of year?"

"I like the fall foliage, but I don't like the way the days get shorter. I miss the sunshine."

"Oh, that's right." Candice laughed. "You're one of those light deprivation people, aren't you? Isn't that called SADS? What does that mean anyway? That you're sad all the time?"

Before Gwen could answer, Candice was introducing her to a slightly bald man who looked to be at least fifteen years older than Gwen. "Willis is with Hadley and Gunderson but Gary has been trying to get him to join forces with him. You know Samuel Green is getting ready to retire."

"So, I take it that means you specialize in criminal law?" said Gwen politely.

"Not exactly. But before I came here I worked for the DA in Brandon. And criminal law has always fascinated me."

"I'm always curious about that," Gwen said as she studied his slightly puffy face. "It's hard to understand why someone wants to defend criminals."

"Oh, no," Candice said with mock horror. "Don't get her

going on that subject, Willis. I completely forgot about her crusade against criminal lawyers. I won't even let her and Gary discuss this anymore."

Willis grinned. "I'm not worried, Candice. I'm a lawyer. Arguing is what I do for a living."

"I suppose you can hold your own then." Candice laughed and began to mingle again.

"So, I take it you are not fond of attorneys who defend criminals?"

Gwen shook her head. "That's not exactly true. I completely agree that everyone has the right to a fair trial. And I think there are cases, especially when innocent people are accused of criminal acts, when the sharpest lawyers are needed. But I've seen some lawyers who skew or even obscure truth and justice just to keep their clients out of jail. Innocence or guilt don't seem to come into play a lot of the time. Take O. J. Simpson—"

"So you think the Juice is guilty?"

"Doesn't everyone?"

"The jury didn't seem to." Willis smiled. He reminded Gwen of a lion licking his chops just before he devoured his prey.

Just as they were thoroughly embroiled, it was time to sit down to dinner. Thankfully, Candice had not arranged the seating, and Gwen managed to politely slip away from Willis and sit by Mary Powers.

"So, did you get the job?" Mary asked as she passed the rolls.

"We're going to give it a try," said Gwen. "We've agreed that if it doesn't work out, we will remain friends."

"That sounds like a wise plan. And if it works out, you can thank me by taking me out to lunch."

"It's a deal," agreed Gwen. She liked Mary. It would be fun

to get better acquainted with her.

For the rest of the evening, Gwen managed to avoid Willis. She was tired of arguing with him. And he reminded her of the defense lawyer who had defended the drunken driver who had killed David. That had been just over a year ago, but it was during the trial that she had begun to question the ethics and morals of criminal lawyers. Although the defendant had been driving with a suspended license, due to other drunk-driving convictions, he had only been charged with manslaughter. But even so, his attorney had managed to get him off with what seemed a mere slap on the hand.

Finally, the crowd began to thin a little, and Gwen told Candice and Gary thank you and good night.

"I hope my friend Willis didn't get your dander up," teased Gary as he walked Gwen to the front porch.

"No, I probably irritated him more than he did me."

"Say, Candice told me you're coming to work for her. Are you sure you can stand working in the same building as a criminal law firm?" Gary was smiling, but Gwen could hear the seriousness in his voice.

Gwen answered lightly. "We'll just have to set some ground rules, Gary. I won't bug you if you don't bug me."

Gary laughed. "Shall I write up an official agreement?"

"No, I think a handshake will do. Thanks again, Gary. It was a fun evening. Even sparring with Willis was sort of interesting in a weird way."

Gwen walked home alone. She knew almost every neighbor on the street, and her house was only a block away. She and David had purchased their home just before Aubrey started first grade. Several years later, Candice and Gary Mallard moved in down the street. At first Gwen had been delighted to have an old friend so nearby. But before long, she realized that

Gary and David could hardly tolerate one another. So up until the last two years, Gwen had rarely socialized with the Mallards or their friends. David had always called them yuppie social climbers. And David was too down-to-earth to go in for such things. Not that Gwen had been overly eager to befriend the Mallards. But Candice, with all her faults, was rather fun and outgoing. And after several hot confrontations with Gary, Gwen had learned to avoid conversations like the one she had shared with Willis tonight.

Gwen unlocked the door and let herself into her house. She had been careful to leave on the porch light as well as several interior lights. As she closed the door behind her, she sighed. Ah, so good to be home. Her house felt light and airy, especially after being in the Mallard's dark home. Gwen kicked off her shoes and sank into the soft, white chenille sofa. It wasn't until Aubrey had started high school that they had gotten white furniture. Up until then, Gwen had wanted a child-friendly home. Not that it was unfriendly now. There were plenty of vibrant splotches of color on pillows and throws and other accent pieces. And Aubrey had always enjoyed their home. But now Aubrey was gone.

Gwen picked up the phone and dialed the number that she already knew by heart.

"Hi, Aubrey. How's it going?"

"Fine, Mom. What's up?"

"Oh, I just wanted to hear your voice."

"Uh-huh," said Aubrey. She sounded different, slightly distant.

"Is everything okay, honey?"

"Yes, Mom." Gwen could hear the trace of irritation in her daughter's voice. "You've called me *every single day* this week, Mom. Is this going to go on all year?"

"No, sweetheart. I'm sorry. It's just that I miss you so much.

And this was your first week at school."

"I know, Mom. And I miss you too. But it's not like I moved out of the state. I'm only a twenty-minute drive away. I'm just hoping that you're not going to call me every night."

"I won't. After this week, I'll be better. I promise." Gwen's voiced brightened. "But I did have a piece of news for you, unless you're too busy to listen." She carefully placed her words before Aubrey like a tasty piece of bait.

"No, Mom, I'm not busy. What is it?"

"Well, I'm going to go to work."

"Good for you, Mom!" Aubrey sounded sincerely glad. "What are you going to do?"

"I'm going to work for Candice Mallard."

"Interior design?"

"Yes, she's needing help. And we're going to try it out and see how it goes."

"Oh, Mom, that's the best news. I'm so happy for you. You're a great interior decorator. Everyone says so. You are going to be so happy!"

Aubrey's happy words were like a tonic to her heart. "I'm excited about it, too. A little nervous though."

"Well, don't be. I think you're way more talented than Candice."

Gwen laughed. "Well, you're my daughter, so you'd have to say that. Just don't say it to anyone else."

"No, really, Mom. Her house is so gloomy and dark. Everything seems old and way too traditional. But the things you do with interiors are always exciting and full of life. Like my room, Mom. All my friends thought it was way cool. In fact, I miss it a little."

"You do?" Gwen smiled. "Thanks, Aubrey. I think I needed to hear that."

"When do you go to work?"

"Monday. And I'm already getting the first-day jitters."

"Well, call me Monday night and tell me how it goes."

"You don't mind if I call you then?"

"Well, as long as you can hold yourself back a little and not call me *every* night. I don't want the girls in the dorm to think I'm a mommy's girl."

Gwen laughed. "Don't worry, Aubrey. I don't think anyone would ever think that of you." Gwen imagined her beautiful, almost six-foot-tall daughter.

"Well, the girls are getting ready to make an ice cream run. I don't want them to leave without me."

"I won't keep you then, Aubrey. Have fun." Gwen was about to hang up. Getting ready, once again, to cut the umbilical cord.

"Hey, I've got an idea, Mom," said Aubrey suddenly. "Want to go shopping this weekend? I could help you pick out some work clothes."

"I'd love it, Aubrey. Do you really want to?"

"Sure, it'd be fun. I'll meet you at the campus Starbuck's at ten on Saturday. Then we can head into Seattle. Okay?"

"Sounds great! Thanks, Aubrey."

Gwen hung up the phone and leaned back into the couch. *This was exciting!* For the first time in ages, she felt that old creative flame within her beginning to flicker. It felt almost as if she might at last be emerging from a long, dark tunnel of winter. She closed her eyes and whispered a heartfelt thanks to God. She had tried to rest in the assurance that he had been holding her in his hand all this time, but often she had felt isolated and forgotten. Now it seemed a new door was opening for her.

TWO

Gwen spent Sunday evening reorganizing her closet. Jeans and casual clothes were relegated to one side, the side that used to be David's, and business clothing was hung on the other. She was going to be a working woman now, and she needed to look like one. Aubrey had been great on their shopping expedition; her instincts for fashion were amazing. If Aubrey ever wanted to give up sports she could probably enter the fashion industry fairly easily. And Gwen knew it wasn't just a mother's bias. Others noticed Aubrey's height, good looks, and strong sense of style, and she had been asked about runway modeling more than once in the last couple years.

Gwen sighed. Life was funny. It seemed like only yesterday Gwen had been teaching Aubrey about these things. Now here she was hanging up the new designer suit that Aubrey had insisted was a must. At first, Gwen had pleaded that she never wore brown, but once she tried it on she knew that Aubrey was right. Aubrey hadn't been too impressed with the dark red wool blazer that Gwen had picked out, but Gwen had convinced her that she needed something perky, too. Finally, Aubrey conceded that people actually wore brown and red together these days, and it might be interesting with the brown skirt. Gwen had also purchased an oatmeal-colored tweed suit that was cut in a very youthful style. She had been slightly concerned that the skirt was a bit on the short side, but Aubrey had insisted that with colored hose and Gwen's great legs it would be perfect. Gwen chuckled as she remembered that. To think that Aubrey thought her old mom had "great legs" was rather amusing. They had also picked out some accessories and shoes, and finally Aubrey had talked Gwen into getting her hair cut. Gwen had never worn her hair shorter than her shoulders, but once again Aubrey had been right. The short style framed her face perfectly and made her delicate features seem more prominent and dramatic.

Gwen closed her closet door with satisfaction and turned to the stack of interior design magazines that she had piled on her bed. After church, she had stopped by the bookstore and picked up all the latest fall issues, everything from *Modern Accent* to *Country Home*. She planned to cram tonight. She wanted to be up on the very latest. Fortunately, as she flipped through the big glossy pages, it didn't seem that much was new or even surprising. David used to always say that there was nothing new under the sun, and she supposed he was right. But she knew that a creative person could take the ordinary things and turn them into something delightful and unexpected. And that's what she wanted to do. She drifted to sleep studying a great room that had been redesigned to accommodate arts-and-crafts-style furnishings. And when she awoke it was morning.

She dressed carefully in the oatmeal-colored suit with a fine gauge silk sweater under the neatly fitted jacket. She fastened a thin brown leather belt around her slim waist and slipped her feet into a pair of shoes the same color, then looked in the mirror. Very nice. Candice wouldn't need to be ashamed of her. She left her house twenty minutes earlier than necessary in order to pick up fresh bagels to share at work. Food was always such a warm way to make new friends.

She had never been to Candice's office before. She had driven by it often enough on the street, but for some reason she had always felt too intimidated to actually drop in and say hello. It was an impressive building from the outside. Originally built in the thirties, it had been refaced during the sixties, but when Candice and Gary purchased it several years back, they had spent a fortune having the exterior restored back to its original art deco style. They had even won an award for it. Gwen assumed that the interior would also be art deco. She wasn't terribly fond of that style, but at least it was usually somewhat clean and light with smooth marble and sleek surfaces.

She parked in the back of the building just as Candice had told her to do. She didn't see Candice's navy Jaguar in the lot and was relieved that she might be able to look around a little before Candice arrived.

"Can I help you?" said a young woman in the hallway as Gwen entered through the back door. She looked at Gwen curiously, obviously wondering why she had entered through the back instead of the front. "Are you here to see someone in the law firm?"

Gwen laughed. "No. I suppose that would be the natural assumption when someone comes sneaking in the back door this early in the morning."

The woman didn't laugh. "Are you here to see Candice then?"

"No, I'm sorry. Let me explain. I'm a friend of Candice's. She probably hasn't had a chance to tell anyone since we only decided this on Friday night. I am to be an employee. Candice has hired me. My name is Gwen Sullivan."

The woman nodded and smiled. "Oh, I get it. Well, I'm Lucinda, and I'm the receptionist here, both for Candice and the law firm upstairs. I usually open the place up at eight, unlock the doors, make coffee, turn on the lights, you know the bit."

Gwen glanced at Lucinda's casual-looking pants and baggy sweater. Her hair hung limply down her back. She looked more like a college kid than a receptionist. "Nice to meet you, Lucinda." She held up her bag of bagels. "I brought some bagels and muffins to share. Maybe I could put them near the coffee."

"Sure. You want the tour before it gets too busy? I just need to stay close enough to answer the phone. Everyone else doesn't get here until nine or later, depending on their moods. Except for Sharon, the bookkeeper—she should be here any minute now."

"I'd love a tour, if you don't mind." Gwen looked around with interest. The place was nothing like she had imagined. Instead of art deco, it was very traditional with oriental carpets, heavy furnishings, and lots of large plants in front of the windows. It reminded Gwen of Candice's home. And, like Candice's home, the office seemed very dark. But perhaps Lucinda hadn't turned on all the lights yet, and of course, the shades were still closed.

"This is the coffee room. Let me get a pot going. There are cups in that cupboard by the sink. No dishwasher, so you gotta clean up for yourself."

Gwen watched as Lucinda filled a dark-stained pot without bothering to scrub it out. She was surprised that Candice, a person so consumed with appearances, would hire someone like Lucinda. Not that she didn't seem nice. Just not very professional. But perhaps she was a first-rate receptionist. That's what mattered.

"The bathroom is there." Lucinda pointed to a door at the end of a hallway. "There's another one upstairs, but the guys mostly use it. I guess this one's the ladies' room." She giggled as she led Gwen down another dark hallway with no windows. "That's the sample room," she pointed to a large, messy-looking room with a table in the center surrounded by floor-to-ceiling shelves. Two of the wall shelves were filled with wallpaper books, and the other two were filled with fabric samples, but nothing appeared to be in any order, either with color or style. "It needs a little work in here," said Lucinda apologetically.

"I'm sure it must be difficult with Candice being so busy."

"That room has all the furniture books and catalogs. I don't even know what all of them are for. There sure are a lot though." This room also seemed disorderly. Gwen wondered how Candice could even begin to find anything in here. She followed Lucinda down another hallway that led to the front of the building. "Now up front is where the clients are allowed. That's the lobby over there, and, of course, my desk. And this," Lucinda opened a set of double doors, "is where Candice meets with the clients."

Gwen stared at the spacious, high-ceilinged room. More oriental carpets, heavy antique tables and chairs, large palms in big brass pots, and original oils on the paneled wall. Leather club chairs were nicely arranged by the shaded windows. Everything was in rich dark tones. It looked very expensive. And impressive. And Gwen was certain that was Candice's goal—to impress.

Just then the phone rang, and Lucinda dashed off to her desk. Gwen looked around a little more. There was an elevator in the hallway, but also a large staircase near the front door. Lucinda wrote down a message and hung up the phone. "Candice's office is upstairs, she can show that to you later. Want to see the basement?"

"I guess so. But I don't want to keep you—"

"Hello there," called a voice from in back.

"Oh, that's Sharon. She can show you the basement. Hey, Sharon, come meet our new coworker."

An older woman was hanging her coat in the closet by the door. "New coworker?" she repeated as she closed the door. "So Candice has finally gotten some help? Well, it's about time."

"This is Gwen—uh, I can't remember your last name."

"Sullivan. I'm a friend of Candice's. In fact, we're not sure how this will go. It's not always wise to hire a friend."

"Well, as long as you don't mind a little hard work, there should be no problem." Sharon was looking Gwen over carefully. Her brows were raised in what seemed to be an almost skeptical expression. Suddenly Gwen wondered if her fashionable appearance gave the impression that she was one of those useless women who only considered herself to be office trimming with no intention of really working.

"Oh, believe me, I like to work hard. I get bored if I'm not kept busy."

Sharon laughed. "Well, we can keep you busy enough."

"Gwen brought treats," said Lucinda. "I've already given her the tour—" The phone rang, and Lucinda dashed off to get it again.

"I've had most of the tour," explained Gwen. "She was going to show me the basement. Although I'm not sure why."

"Because some of our office equipment is down there. Let me put my purse in my office and I'll show you. Did you see my office already?"

"No, actually, I didn't."

"No wonder. It's really nothing more than a closet. But at least it has a window. And I keep my shade open."

Gwen looked at Sharon oddly, and Sharon laughed. "Well, you see, Candice has this thing about not opening the blinds. She's afraid the sunlight will fade the carpets. And, as you may know, these carpets are worth a small fortune. So don't be opening any blinds or Candice will have your hide."

Gwen nodded. "That's why it's so dark in here. Are all the lights on?"

"Yes, Lucinda does that first thing in the morning. It is rather dark in here, but you'll get used to it after a while."

Gwen nodded. She was already feeling uncomfortable with the gloomy atmosphere. She wasn't so sure she would get used to it. But she would do her best to try. She followed Sharon down a narrow stairway in the back of the building.

"There's an elevator that goes to the basement, but Candice doesn't want us to use it because it's right where clients come in. Watch yourself on these stairs, they're steep, but you'll get used to them after a while."

The basement smelled damp and moldy. "It seems a little inconvenient to have the office machines down here," said Gwen, trying not to breathe too deeply of the foul-smelling air. "Do you have to come down here much?"

"I try to keep my trips to once or twice a day. It's mostly the copier. It's such a huge monster—this was the only place with enough room for it. It's pretty handy though. It can even copy large floor plans."

"Whose desk is that?" Gwen asked when she spotted a desk in a dark corner.

"No one's right now. Well, I guess that completes your tour. Candice will probably get here in the next hour or so, depending on her appointment schedule. And I am in need of a cup of coffee."

"That sounds good," said Gwen. "And I picked up some pumpkin muffins with the bagels."

"Well, Gwen, it looks as if you're off to a good start," said Sharon with a smile. "If there's anything I can do to help you

27

get better adjusted, just feel free to ask. I've been with Candice since she opened her doors, and I know a lot about this place."

"Thanks, Sharon. I appreciate that. How long has Lucinda been here? She doesn't seem very old."

"She's been here a little over a year. She has a toddler who's in child care. She's a single mom. Gary hired her. She was involved with one of his clients, if you know what I mean, and I think Gary felt sorry for her and wanted to give her a chance at a better life. So far so good."

"That's nice," said Gwen. "Really nice."

Gwen poked around for a while until Candice finally came in. But when Candice arrived she barely spoke to Gwen. She just breezed right through and began shouting commands to Sharon and Lucinda and then headed up to her office. Gwen blinked in surprise as she watched the back of Candice's long coat flap behind her as she dashed up the stairs. Candice didn't even offer to show Gwen her office.

Gwen turned to Sharon. "Is something wrong?"

Sharon chuckled. "No. This is typical. We sometimes call her Hurricane Candice. She whips through here and leaves all sorts of devastation in her wake. But we usually have it cleaned up by the time she comes back down. She is a wonderful person but not the best communicator and not the best organizer. That's why she needs a good team. Welcome to the team, Gwen."

"But what am I supposed to do?"

"Well, there's plenty to be done. How about if I make a list for starters? Then when Candice has time, she can get you going on her projects. You said you don't mind hard work, right?"

By midafternoon, Gwen was almost sorry she had said she didn't mind hard work. It seemed that Sharon was determined to turn her into a moving man. But Gwen was equally determined not to disappoint anyone. Sharon told Gwen that

Candice wanted to move her office downstairs and needed the sample room cleared out so she could set up in there. So Gwen went out and got boxes and spent most of the day packing and toting heavy boxes down to the basement where new shelves had already been constructed for the samples. It seemed she had barely made a dent on the job, but she was dog-tired and had blisters on her heels from carefully navigating up and down those steep stairs. She must have made a hundred trips and considered it no small miracle that she had not fallen and seriously injured herself.

Gwen had no hopes of talking to her new boss since Candice had left for a job two hours away without even saying a word to her. Gwen's only hope was to survive the day, and perhaps tomorrow would be better.

"You are doing great," Sharon said when she came down to the basement to make some copies. "Those shelves look so neat. Much better than when they were upstairs. Now maybe Candice will be able to find things more easily."

"I hope so," said Gwen, trying to sound cheerful. "But at this rate, I think it will take all week to complete this task."

"Well, that's not so bad. I had told Candice that I thought it would take at least a week and a half. You're already ahead of schedule."

Gwen smiled weakly and sighed. The truth was she didn't know if she could last a whole week at this rate. This was hard manual labor. But still she was determined not to fail. Not yet. This was her chance. She would give it her all.

That night, after a hot soak in the tub and a microwave dinner, Gwen called Aubrey. "Hi, honey. I don't want to bother you, but you did tell me to call."

"How did it go today, Mom?" Aubrey sounded sincerely interested. "Did you impress Candice with your stylish new image?"

Gwen laughed. "Candice didn't even give me the time of day."

"What? Why not?" Aubrey was indignant.

"Oh, she was busy. And I had a job to do." Gwen didn't want to go into all the dreary details. She felt humiliated by the day and didn't want Aubrey to know.

"But do you *like* it?"

"Like it?" Gwen's voice sounded too high. "Well, I think it's too soon to know for sure, honey. But I plan on giving it my all. It certainly wasn't glamorous. It was just plain, hard work, and I'm literally exhausted right now."

"That's too bad, Mom. Do you think that Candice is just testing you? Sort of like freshman initiation?"

Gwen thought about that for a long moment. "Maybe so, Aubrey. Well, like I said, I'll give it my all. That's all I can do."

"That's the spirit, Mom. Hang in there, old girl."

Gwen groaned. "I sure do feel like an old girl tonight."

"The first day has got to be the toughest. It'll get better."

Before Gwen fell asleep, she prayed for strength to make it through the next day. She had often prayed for emotional strength, but now she prayed for both emotional and physical strength. She also prayed that she would work for Candice just as if she were working for the Lord. That had always been her goal when she had managed the design department at Sullivan's Furniture. And it had always seemed to work.

The next morning, Gwen arrived at work at eight o'clock sharp, just as Lucinda was unlocking the doors. Today Gwen had dressed in neat khaki pants with a chambray shirt, utilizing her red blazer and a designer scarf to give her a more professional appearance. But her goal today was to be able to remove her jacket, roll up her sleeves, and really work. And she had a plan to speed things up. Yesterday, she had noticed a large laundry cart in the basement. She hoped to load the cart with lots of samples and make several trips in the elevator before anyone else arrived to notice or be bothered.

Thankfully Lucinda thought it was a fine idea. Gwen went right to work and managed to unload an entire wall of fabric samples before anyone else came to work. In order to be quick about her work she had simply dumped the samples all over the basement floor by the shelves. It looked pretty chaotic, but no one used that part of the basement and the fabric all needed to be sorted and refolded anyway. Gwen was sitting in the midst of the mess when Candice came down to the basement.

"What in the world are you doing?" Candice cried when she saw Gwen knee deep in fabric samples.

Gwen looked up and laughed. "I know it looks dreadful right now, but don't worry, everything's under control."

Candice didn't look convinced. "Well, I certainly hope so." She handed Gwen a stack of floor-plan drawings. "Make me two sets of copies of these and bring them up to my office right away."

"Sure," said Gwen, standing and brushing lint from her pants.

Candice frowned at her and Gwen wished she hadn't taken off her blazer. She knew her appearance didn't look very professional right now.

"I just hope this wasn't a big mistake," Candice muttered as she turned and went up the stairs.

Gwen echoed the sentiment as she went over to the big copy machine. She knew how to make regular-sized copies, but she wasn't sure about these oversized pieces. She had always depended on the office girls at the furniture store to do these types of things for her. But how hard could it possibly be? After several failed attempts, Gwen decided that either this machine didn't like her, or she was just plain stupid. She ran upstairs to see if perhaps Sharon could help.

"You don't know how to use a copier?" Sharon said in a slightly exasperated tone.

"Well, not for these larger-sized pieces. I thought I was doing it right, but the copier just isn't cooperating."

"Well, let me finish up and save this." Sharon turned to her computer and worked for several more minutes. Gwen wished she would hurry since Candice had said "right away," but she didn't want to push Sharon.

Finally Sharon went down to the basement and launched into what turned out to be a lengthy lecture on how to use the copy machine. Gwen tried to sound patient as she jotted down notes, knowing that this was probably her only chance to get this lesson. At last, she had the sets of copies in hand, but before she went up to Candice's office, she slipped on her jacket and adjusted her scarf. Hopefully she might make a better impression this time.

"Good grief," exclaimed Candice. "What took you so long?"

"I had to get Sharon to give me a lesson on the copier—"

Candice scowled. "You mean you don't know how to use a copy machine?"

"Well, yes and no. But I do now." Gwen tried to smile.

"I wonder what else you don't know how to do," Candice mumbled as she took the copies.

"I think you'll find I'm a fast learner," said Gwen, afraid that she sounded defensive. "And there's a whole lot I know that you won't have to teach me."

Candice waved her hand as if dismissing her. "Yeah, I'm

sure there is. But right now I'm expecting a client, and I need to get some things together. Just when do you expect to have that sample room empty anyway?"

Gwen felt like screaming, but instead she calmly said, "It's coming along as fast as it can. Perhaps you'd like me to hire some extra help to get things moving quicker."

"That's why I hired you," Candice said, not bothering to mask her exasperation.

"Well, I hope to be done in the next couple days. I'll let you get back to your work now." Gwen turned and walked away. Hot tears of humiliation burned in her eyes, but she would not cry. Instead she returned to the basement and began systematically sorting and folding fabric samples with a vengeance. By noon she had the fabric all neatly put away. She stepped back and admired her work.

"That looks real nice, Gwen," said Sharon from the stairs. "After you take your lunch I have some errands for you to run."

Gwen spent the afternoon being a gofer. She picked up some custom drapes, dropped off a print to be framed, stopped by the warehouse to locate a floor lamp, and finally picked up Candice's dry cleaning. She had never liked driving in town, but she decided that moving through traffic and looking for parking places was less exhausting than carrying loads of heavy wallpaper books down to the basement.

As Gwen drove back to the office, she thought about how this job was not turning out to be anything like she had expected. Perhaps it was all a big mistake after all. But as dismal as it seemed, there was still something inside her that didn't want to give up. She wasn't sure if she wanted to prove something to Candice or to herself. But no matter how difficult it was, Gwen was determined to give it everything she had.

THREE

The evening following her second day of work, Gwen felt more than just physically exhausted; she felt completely discouraged. She wondered if working in the light-deprived environment was beginning to take its toll on her. She walked around her own house in her stocking feet, turning on every single light. She even lit some candles. Then she put on a favorite CD of light classics, collapsed on the couch, and tried to feel better.

Alone. She felt so very much alone. She looked at the phone, longing to call Aubrey but knowing that she could not. She had promised to ease up on her daily phone calls, and she had just spoken to her last night. She took a deep breath and leaned her head back into the soft couch. Perhaps this was what Candice had called "empty-nest syndrome." Although Gwen had denied it at the time, it felt very real right now. Painfully real.

But it wasn't fair. Most women who suffered from empty-nest syndrome probably still had a husband. She thought about her good friend Jana. Jana's youngest daughter, a friend of Aubrey, had just left to go to school out of state. At least Jana still had her husband. Still Jana might understand a bit of what Gwen was feeling. Maybe she should give her a call. Gwen glanced at her watch. It was the dinner hour. Not a good time for a chat.

Gwen went into the kitchen and looked blankly at the milky white cabinets with their leaded-glass doors. She ran her

35

hand over the cool, green marble countertop, perfect for rolling out pastry. She had redesigned their kitchen several years back because it seemed to be the one place where their little family spent most of their time. Those were happy times. It was hard to believe that only two years ago, the three of them had gathered in here, laughing and joking and sharing about the events of the day.

She had planned the little sink in the breakfast bar in order to accommodate the salad chef, usually David. He had always managed to concoct the most imaginative salads, never afraid to combine unusual ingredients, things like asparagus and prunes, and his dressings were always incredible. Too bad he never had a chance to write them down for her.

For Aubrey, Gwen had designed a special baking center. Aubrey had been the designated baker—she made a chocolate hazelnut cake that was heavenly. And Gwen had always been content to fill in the rest of the menu. She often heard friends complain about fixing dinner every night, but she had never minded cooking with her loved ones close by. It had always been a part of the day that she looked forward to.

She hadn't cooked a real thing since Aubrey had left for college. She didn't even like going into the kitchen. And so she lived on microwave meals, canned soup, and fresh fruit. She hadn't intended it to be like this. She had never been the type of person to eat from cans and boxes, but whenever she stepped into the kitchen it felt so empty—almost haunted—that the most she could do was to quickly heat something then take it into the living room to eat.

Tonight was no different. She opened a can of chicken and rice soup, dumped it into a bowl, and punched the soup button on the microwave. As this heated, she popped a piece of whole wheat bread in the toaster and waited, drumming her fingers on the counter. Then she arranged her bleak dinner on an enamel tray and carried it out into the brightly lit living room. She set the tray on the coffee table, sat down, and burst into tears. Why was this so hard? She allowed herself to sob for a while, thinking that a good cry might wash away this unwanted melancholy. And then she allowed herself to travel down memory lane, hoping that some old event, perhaps even something that she had done wrong, might shed some light on her lonely situation.

All her life, it seemed as if she had tried to do everything right. As a child, she had been obedient and thoughtful. She had never even gone through a rebellious period. She had always gone to church and gotten good grades in school. Compared to her older sister, Leslie, Gwen had been the "good daughter." Not that she had relished that distinction, but it was as if she could do nothing else. Leslie used to tease and call her Little Goody Gwenny, and there were times when Gwen had actually wanted to be bad if only to show Leslie that she could.

But the fact was *she couldn't.* Not really. Her father used to brag that Gwen was incapable of doing anything wrong. And as much as it irritated her, she knew it was mostly true. Of course, her parents had appreciated it, especially when Leslie had gone the hippie route and gotten involved with drugs and all that went with them. Gwen had even felt sorry for her sister, wondering if perhaps Gwen hadn't been so good, maybe Leslie wouldn't have needed to be so bad. Fortunately, Leslie had gotten her life straightened out—mostly.

Even when Gwen had decided not to finish college in order to marry at age nineteen, it wasn't considered a bad thing. Her parents had always loved her high-school sweetheart, David Sullivan, and supported the couple in their choice to marry by throwing a big church wedding with all the trimmings. Her dad had said it was a whole lot better than all the "shacking up" that kids were doing back then. In an age of accepted sexual promiscuity, Gwen had self-consciously concealed the fact that both she and David were virgins until their wedding night. Aubrey was born just after their first anniversary. And in nearly seventeen years of marriage, David and Gwen had never cheated on each other—an amazing feat these days.

Gwen replayed those happy years of being David's wife and Aubrey's mom. She had continued working hard to do things right. She'd been the Brownie troop leader, president of the PTA, and active in the church. She had planted bulbs in the fall and annuals in the spring. She hadn't even worked outside the home until Aubrey was eleven, and then only part-time at the furniture store during the hours that Aubrey was in school. Gwen had enjoyed the work, and she knew she had been good at it, but it was never more important to her than her little family. She and David had wanted more children, but for some reason that the doctors could never determine, it hadn't happened. But even then, Gwen had committed herself to be content. If God only wanted her to have one child, then she would love that one child with everything she had. And she worked even harder not to smother her independent little daughter with all her love.

So, why then, when she had tried to do everything so right, had it all turned out so wrong? Here she was only thirty-eight years old, in the prime of life, but she felt old and worn, used up and useless, and lonely. Incredibly lonely. She didn't really mean to question God, but it just didn't seem fair. What was the use of working so hard if this was all you got in the end? What was it all for? Maybe she should just give up. Maybe she should just quit trying so hard to do everything so right. Fresh tears poured down her cheeks. She didn't want to give up. She didn't even know how. It would be easier to stop breathing.

Just then the phone rang. She took a deep breath and tried to purge the sob out of her voice before she answered.

"Hi, Gwen. I know you're probably just sitting down to eat, but I was thinking of you and thought I'd give you a quick jingle. How are you doing?"

Gwen sniffed. "Your timing is pretty good, Mom. I was just falling apart."

"What's wrong, sweetheart?"

Gwen sighed. "Just the blues, I guess. It's hard being all alone in the house. I guess you must understand—did you feel like that after Daddy died?"

"Of course. That's why I sold the house and moved into the condo. That was the smartest thing to do. And I'm grateful to you for encouraging me to do it. I've got so many friends now. Maybe you should think about—"

"No," interrupted Gwen. She was definitely not ready for condo living. "I really like my house, and the memories are good ones. But sometimes it's hard."

"So tell me, how is the new job going?"

Gwen groaned. "Don't ask."

"What's wrong?"

"It's just not what I expected, I guess. I really don't want to give up, but I'm afraid it might have been a mistake."

"But why? You are so talented at decorating. And you and Candice are such good friends."

"We're not that good of friends, Mom. And it doesn't look like I'm going to get to do much decorating. I think she needed an errand girl more than anything."

"That's too bad, dear. Maybe you should think about starting your own business."

Gwen laughed. "I wish! But I don't think that would be possible."

"Well, I have friends here at the condo who would hire you. I could spread the word around."

"Thanks, Mom." Gwen smiled. Her mom had such a way of oversimplifying things. She had no idea what went into starting a decorating firm. "If I ever decide to hang out my shingle, you'll be the first one to know."

"Well, I believe you could do it, sweetheart."

"Thanks, Mom. It's nice to know someone believes in me."

"Don't let this get to you, Gwennie. You know what they say about it being the darkest before the dawn. Maybe Candice is just breaking you in. Maybe she really plans to use your decorating skills, but she wants to see how serious you are about work."

"Maybe. Aubrey suggested the same thing."

"How is Aubrey?"

"She's doing just great. I'm the one who keeps getting into trouble for calling her too much."

Her mother laughed. "She's always been such an independent little thing!"

"Yes, but I miss her."

"I know, dear. But give her time to feel her independence, and then she'll probably be calling you."

"That sounds like sage advice from someone who's been there."

Her mother chuckled again. "That's right. And that should remind you that you can always call me, too. You can't always depend on my 'perfect timing,' you know."

"Thanks, Mom. I'll try to remember that. Thanks for calling."

Gwen's soup was cold now, but she ate it anyway. Then she went to bed.

The next day, she arrived at work at eight o'clock sharp

again. Her goal was to use the laundry cart and elevator to get all the wallpaper books down to the basement before nine o'clock. Then perhaps she could finish this horrible task and move on to something more interesting. If this were just a test, she was determined to pass it.

Lucinda was smoking a cigarette when Gwen walked in, and she quickly snuffed it out. "You're sure an early bird," she said with a guilty look.

"I wanted to use the elevator again this morning," said Gwen. "I'm hoping to have that room all cleared out today."

"That should make Candice happy. And when Candice is happy, we're all happy."

Gwen sensed a sarcastic edge to Lucinda's voice but didn't want to waste any precious time before nine. She went right to work, moving as fast as she could—up and down the elevator. It was just a couple minutes past nine as she was pushing her last load into the elevator, when Gary Mallard walked in the front door. He looked at Gwen in surprise.

"And what have we here?" he asked with a puzzled brow.

"I'm emptying the sample room so Candice can set up her office," explained Gwen breathlessly. "I was using the elevator before business hours so—"

"It's business hours right now."

"I suppose so," said Gwen. "This is the last load. Sorry." She went into the elevator and pushed the down button and sighed. It would be nice to feel just a little appreciation here. Pushing those thoughts aside, she went right to work organizing the sample books and adjusting the shelf bracket heights to make sure everything fit just right. It was almost noon when she finished. She couldn't believe it—she was done! She knew it was only a small thing, but she had really done a great job, and in half the time expected. And not only did it look nice

41

and neat, but it would be very efficient and easy to use.

"Are you down here, Gwen?" called Candice from the stairs.

"Yes," answered Gwen cheerfully. "I'm just finishing up."

"Well, that's good," said Candice, barely bothering to look at the shelves. "Gary mentioned that you were using the elevator—"

"Yes, I'm sorry. But now I'm finished. And it cut the time in half."

"Well, please don't do it again, Gwen. Gary said you looked like a bag lady wheeling your grocery cart—not a very good image for the firm."

Gwen felt her cheeks heat up. A bag lady indeed!

"And I noticed it looks pretty bad in the old sample room," continued Candice as if chastising a small child. "Everything is all dusty, and there's lint all over the carpet."

"Yes, well, I haven't had a chance to clean it up. I wanted to get these things put away down here first so they wouldn't be all over the floor."

Candice frowned. "Then please get to it right away, Gwen."

Gwen stared in amazement as Candice headed back up the stairs. Did Candice think that Gwen was her personal slave? Gwen didn't have to take this. In fact, there was no reason she couldn't just march right out of here. But then Gwen had never been a quitter. And she wasn't ready to start now. Especially after she had just finished this horrible task.

Instead of going to lunch at noon, Gwen stayed and cleaned the old sample room until it was literally shining. She carefully vacuumed the Persian carpet. She found wood oil and gave the shelves a good rubdown. She even dusted the hanging lights—they looked like they hadn't been touched in ages. Finally, she stepped back and smiled in satisfaction. This would make a nice office if it only had windows. Surely Candice wouldn't be able to complain about this. Then Gwen went out to have some lunch.

When she got back, Sharon was waiting by the back door with a dark frown. "Where have you been?" she demanded, looking at her watch.

"To lunch. Candice wanted me to get the sample room cleaned up, and I didn't leave until almost one, and I only took forty minutes for lunch. What's wrong?"

"Candice needed you to go on a job with her and do some measuring, but you weren't here. She waited until one-thirty, and then left in a huff."

"It's too bad she didn't mention it earlier. Perhaps I should go and meet her there," said Gwen. She sighed. No matter what she did, it was all wrong.

"No. Candice said since you weren't here on time, you could start moving some old files down to the basement for me."

Gwen stared at Sharon in amazement. Was this meant to be her punishment? "Just how much stuff do you guys need moved to the basement anyway?"

Sharon laughed. "Are you complaining?"

"Not really." Gwen put her purse in the closet. "I guess I thought this job was going to be more than just grunt work."

"Well, we've been running shorthanded around here for a long time, and consequently a lot of things have fallen by the wayside. Besides, we all have to start somewhere. Nothing wrong with a little grunt work. You'll need to go to an office supply store and pick up some banker's boxes. And while you're out, here's a list of errands that Candice needs done." Sharon handed her a slip of paper.

By the end of the day, Gwen had gotten Sharon's files safely stowed downstairs and still had enough time left over to begin organizing the furniture and light fixture catalogs. No one had told her to do it, but it obviously needed doing. Candice never came back to the office, but Gwen didn't really care. She wasn't eager to be scolded again.

As Gwen grouped the leather furniture catalogs together, she thought about what her mother had said last night about setting up her own decorating firm. How hard could it really be? But as quickly as the thought came, she dismissed it. Who would want to hire her? She wasn't properly trained. She didn't have any fancy degrees to hang on her walls. Sure, she had good instincts, but how do you sell instinct?

That night Gwen picked up some Chinese food and a video of an old classic movie on her way home. She never even went into the kitchen. She used the complimentary bamboo chopsticks and ate right out of the white cartons as she watched the movie. David had never approved of people eating in front of the TV. He said it was uncivilized, and at the time Gwen had wholeheartedly agreed. But for some reason it didn't seem to matter anymore. The movie was a bit of a disappointment, and before it even ended, she had fallen asleep on the comfortable couch.

FOUR

Gwen dressed carefully on Thursday morning, her fourth day on the job. It seemed the majority of the grunt work must be out of the way by now, and she hoped to have a word with Candice. And to do so, she wanted to look professional and confident. She chose the brown designer suit that Aubrey had insisted was a must. It was just the sort of suit that Candice would appreciate—it said *success*. Perhaps they would discuss exactly what Gwen's role was and what her future might be working for Candice. Gwen knew that she could probably learn a lot from Candice—if Candice was willing to teach her. That was what she hoped to discover today. She knotted a dark paisley scarf around her throat and studied her image in the mirror. Very professional.

Candice didn't come into the office all morning, so Gwen kept herself busy organizing the catalog room. She took her time with the catalogs, studying the different manufacturers, trying to reacquaint herself with the looks and styles of various companies. Some of the companies hadn't been carried at Sullivan's Furniture and were new to her. But many of them were quite familiar, and it was reassuring to recall their strengths and weaknesses, which ones delivered promptly, and which ones were willing to make changes. She knew that her knowledge could be an asset to Candice, if only Candice would give her a chance to prove it. Sharon had informed Gwen that Candice was supposed to be in by noon, so Gwen decided to skip lunch in order not to miss her again today.

"Since you're not going to lunch today," began Sharon, "I wonder if you could do me a favor?"

Gwen slid an outdoor furniture catalog onto a shelf and turned around. "What's that, Sharon?"

"Well, as you know, I usually watch the reception desk while Lucinda takes her lunch, and we take turns for who goes out first. But if you wouldn't mind watching the front desk, I could use the extra time to pick up a birthday present for my grandson."

Gwen smiled. "Sure, just show me what to do. I didn't know you had a grandson, Sharon."

"Oh, I have five grandkids. But between you and me, Aaron is my favorite—he's turning five this weekend. And I want to find something special."

Sharon showed Gwen the basics of the reception desk just as Lucinda was leaving, and it seemed simple enough, but Gwen jotted down some notes on how to use the many phone lines just in case.

"You won't have to transfer any calls since everyone is already at lunch, so it shouldn't be difficult." Sharon got her purse. "Thanks, Gwen, I appreciate it."

Gwen sat down at the desk and looked over her notes. No big deal. After a couple minutes a call came in for Gary, and she jotted down the message and hung up. She picked up a *People* magazine that Lucinda must have been reading and absently thumbed through it when the door opened. She looked up and smiled as a tall, athletic-looking young man walked into the office. He had on jeans and a black leather jacket. He was an attractive man in a dark, sultry way.

"May I help you?" she asked.

"I need to see Gary," said the man, looking up the stairs.

"I'm sorry, Gary's out for lunch right now. But I can give him a message for you."

The man frowned. "Okay. Just tell him that T. J. Thompson wants to talk to him right away. He knows my number." The man looked around the office. "It looks pretty deserted in here."

Gwen smiled. "Yes, everyone seems to be at lunch."

T. J. stepped up and planted both hands on her desk. He leaned over and smiled. "And you're new around here."

A little caution flag rose inside her, but she suppressed it. "Yes, I only came to work this week. I'm a friend of Candice Mallard."

He leaned over further, his face inches from hers. "And what's your name?"

She really didn't want to answer. She didn't like his mannerisms, but since she was an employee she supposed she should be polite to everyone. "My name is Gwen," she said coolly.

"Gwen. That's a pretty name." He began to step around her desk, and the movement made her nervous. What was he doing?

"Did you need something?" she asked as she scooted her chair back and stood.

He moved closer and stuck out his hand as if to shake hers. "I just wanted us to have a proper introduction, Gwen. What's your last name?"

She stepped back and bumped into the wall. She had no intention of taking his hand. This felt wrong. All wrong. "My last name is Sullivan, T. J. And right now you are making me a little uncomfortable."

He stepped closer and laughed. "I like making people uncomfortable. You sure are pretty, Gwen." He reached out and planted both hands against the wall on either side of her head. Her heart was pounding with fear now, and her mouth was as dry as sand. She glanced to the right only to see a tattoo of a rose on his large forearm. She swallowed hard and tried to speak.

"I don't know what you think you're doing, T. J., but you need to back off," she said in a shaky voice.

Again he laughed. "And how are you going to make me, Gwen Sullivan?"

She had heard of kicking men in the groin but didn't know if she could do such a thing or if it would even work. Just then the front door opened. T. J.'s arms dropped to his sides, and he stepped back. In the same instant, Gwen burst away from him and dashed for the front door, practically tumbling into the arms of another strange man who had just stepped into the office.

But at least this man looked respectable. He had on a dark suit and tie and looked as surprised as she was frightened. She looked up at him with pleading eyes, as if begging him to help her.

"What's going on here?" he asked, quickly looking over to where T. J. was still sheepishly standing behind the reception desk.

"I was just leaving," T. J. said as he brushed past the two of them and shot out the door.

Gwen felt her knees turn to jelly, and she collapsed on the couch in the waiting room. "Thank God you came in when you did."

He sat down beside her and peered at her face. "Are you okay? What was going on here?"

"Well, I was just watching the reception desk for an hour, and I was all alone and that horrible man came in to see Gary, and then he acted like he was going to do something to me—" Tears began to roll down her cheeks. "And I'm so glad that you came when you did. Thank you."

He handed her a handkerchief and smiled. "Glad to be of service." He glanced around the office. "Actually, I'm surprised that they would leave a woman all alone here."

"Why?" she asked as she dried her tears and tried to compose herself.

"Well, the nature of the law offices upstairs, I suppose. A lot of unsavory people pass through these doors."

"I guess you're right." She handed him back the handkerchief with embarrassment. She felt like she should wash it for him but didn't know what else to do. "Thank you."

"No problem. Are you okay?"

"Yes, just shaken. But what do you think I should do about that man? Are you a lawyer?"

He chuckled. "No, thank goodness." Then turned more serious. "Did the man assault you?"

"Well, no. He just made unwanted advances...."

"In that case I would recommend that you inform Candice and Gary. They need to know they put you in a bad situation."

"That sounds like good advice." She looked at him curiously, and then realized that she was supposed to be manning the reception desk. "And how may I help you? You must have come to the office for a reason other than rescuing me. Are you here to see Gary?"

The man's brows raised mysteriously. "Ah yes, I could be another one of those unsavory clients, couldn't I?"

Gwen suddenly stood up and stepped back, taking a deep breath. *Not again.* She studied him for a long moment. He was an attractive man who, like T. J., had dark good looks. But he wasn't sultry, rather more Mediterranean, except for the dark blue eyes. And of course he was older than T. J., with even a few gray hairs showing at the temples. He really looked harmless, but how was one to know? Was she going to be paranoid over every dark stranger from now on?

"I'm sorry," said the man, his eyes twinkling. "I couldn't resist. Actually, it would be good for you to take this whole thing as a warning; it won't hurt to watch folks a little more carefully from now on, right?"

She nodded, still not sure why he was here. "So why are you here, Mr.—" she stammered. "I don't recall if you told me your name…"

He smiled. "Sorry, under the circumstances it was easy to forget the proper niceties." He stuck out his hand. "I'm Oliver Black, and I have an appointment with Candice at 12:30. I know it's inconvenient, but I had to make it during the lunch hour, and she said that would be fine."

Gwen sighed in relief and shook his hand. "Nice to meet you, Oliver. My name is Gwen Sullivan. And Candice hasn't come in yet. I was expecting her to come at noon. In fact that's why I agreed to watch the front desk because I wanted to speak with her, too."

Oliver looked at his watch and frowned. "Do you think she's coming?"

"I really don't know. Do you want to wait a few minutes?"

He looked at her and smiled. "Sure, if you don't mind."

"Actually, the company would be appreciated. I still have the shakes from that little episode. I don't think I want to be here alone anymore."

He nodded. "I don't think it's wise. So, Gwen, how long have you been working for Candice?"

"Actually, I only started this week. She and I are friends, and we thought we'd give it a try—see how it goes."

"And how is it going?"

Gwen thought for a moment, not wanting to say anything negative since this was a client, or prospective client. "I guess it's going okay. I haven't worked for a couple of years, and it's a bit of a challenge to try and fit in and all."

"I see. Have you worked in interior decorating before?"

She nodded. "Yes. My husband, well he's deceased now, but his family owns Sullivan's Fine Furnishings, and I used to run their design department."

"I'm sorry."

She looked at him, puzzled for a moment. "Oh, you mean about my husband. Yes, it certainly hasn't been easy. Anyway, I really haven't worked since then. But my daughter is just starting college, and I felt I needed something to do—you know to ward off empty-nest syndrome." She tried to laugh, but it sounded more like she was choking.

He shook his head. "I find it incredible that you could have a daughter old enough to be going to college."

She smiled. "I got an early start."

"And do you have other children?"

"No, just Aubrey."

"Aubrey. That's a pretty name."

"Thanks, it was after my grandmother."

They chatted until Lucinda returned at one. And when they stopped, Gwen realized that he had asked most of the questions, and she had given most of the answers. Other than his name, she had learned very little about him.

"Well, I've got another appointment at one-thirty," Oliver said as he stepped toward the door. "Tell Candice I'm sorry I missed her. But it was a pleasure meeting you, Gwen. I'll have my secretary call to reschedule something later."

As soon as Oliver was out of the door, Gwen launched into

the story about T. J. and how badly he had frightened her.

"Oh, don't worry about him, Gwen. T. J. is just a big talker. Gary says that he's perfectly harmless. He pulled something like that on me once, and I put him in his place, and he's never done it again. He just likes getting a rise out of people. Did you know he plays football for the Washington Wolves?"

"No, and I don't really care. I think he is rude and inconsiderate. And I was about to call the police."

Lucinda looked shocked. "Don't ever do that, Gwen. Gary would get mad. These are his clients. If you call the police you could really mess things up."

Gwen stared at Lucinda in disbelief. Was she suggesting that these clients, possible criminals, should have more protection than the employees who worked in this office? Gwen just shook her head and walked away. "I think I'll go and get a sandwich since I haven't had my lunch break yet."

When she returned Sharon and Lucinda were in the midst of a conversation, but they stopped the minute Gwen stepped into earshot.

"I hear T. J. shook you up today," said Sharon lightly.

"It was more than just being shook up," said Gwen with conviction. "I think that man could be dangerous."

Sharon laughed. "He wouldn't hurt a fly—unless it was on the football field. He just likes to jerk people's chains and get reactions from them. Don't worry about T. J."

"Well, one of Candice's clients came in, and he was concerned. He said that he didn't think any of us should be alone in the office."

Lucinda laughed now. "And maybe we should hire a security guard, too."

Gwen stared at the two of them. "Well, I'm sorry, but I was honestly frightened, and I intend to talk to Candice about it."

"Talk to Candice about what?" Candice called as she came in through the back door.

"Hello, Candice," said Sharon cheerfully. "T. J. Thompson dropped in and frightened our little Gwen."

"Really?" Candice said as she set down a box of samples and thumbed through the mail. "Well, T. J. can be a little intimidating, but he's just a big talker. You don't need to take him seriously, Gwen."

Gwen didn't know what to say. She was starting to wonder if she had imagined the whole thing. "Well, Oliver Black didn't seem to think he was harmless."

Candice laid down the mail and turned to face Gwen. "Oliver Black?"

"Yes, he stopped in for an appointment with you, and he was just in time to see T. J. practically attacking me."

"Oh, dear!" exclaimed Candice.

Relief washed over Gwen. She had finally gotten someone's attention. "Yes, it was really quite awkward, but Oliver—"

"Good grief, I can't believe that I totally blanked that appointment. Was he upset? Did he ask me to call him?"

Gwen answered mechanically. "He said that his secretary would call and set something up for another date." Gwen stared at Candice for a moment. It was plain to see that Candice wasn't a bit worried about the T. J. incident. "Candice," began Gwen hesitantly, "I was wondering if I could meet with you today?"

"Not today, Gwen. I have a million things to do. Next week—I promise."

"Okay," said Gwen disheartened. She turned to walk away.

"Hey, Gwen," Candice called in a consoling—or was it patronizing?—tone. "I wanted to tell you that you're doing a good job. That sample room looks much better. The carpenter is coming in this weekend to take out most of those shelves, and hopefully I'll be able to move in my office furniture by the end of next week."

Gwen nodded. She appreciated the compliment but wondered why Candice had made such an issue about having that room cleaned just so a carpenter could come make a mess tearing out the shelves. But she kept her thoughts to herself.

"And as a congratulations for surviving your first week, Sharon has a present for you." Candice nodded to Sharon, and Sharon seemed to understand.

"And if Oliver Black calls," Candice directed this to Lucinda, "put him straight through to me—the whole VIP treatment."

Gwen went back to organizing the catalogs, mildly curious as to what the mysterious congratulations gift might be, but at the same time still irked over their casual attitude over T. J. Thompson's offensive behavior. She wished that she could just let it go, too, but the memory of how T. J. had made her feel like a helpless victim was too vivid and disturbing. And it irritated her that someone like T. J. was freely roaming the streets terrorizing at will. She wondered why he wanted to see Gary. It wouldn't surprise her if he was facing some serious criminal charges. She recalled hearing something not too long ago about some local professional athlete who had gotten into trouble for something or other. She scooted some catalogs tighter to make room for one more.

"How's it coming, Gwen?" asked Sharon.

"Okay. I'm almost finished in here. I'm not sure what I should begin next. It seems like most of the organizing tasks are done now."

Sharon nodded. "You've done a good job, Gwen—a lot faster than I expected. And now I will present you with your little gift." Sharon grinned almost mischievously, and then held out what looked like some sort of key chain.

Gwen took the item in her hand. "Thanks. What is it?"

Sharon laughed. "You mean you've never seen one of these before? Well, handle it with care. It's pepper spray. We all carry them, just in case."

"In case of what?" Gwen looked at Sharon suspiciously.

"Well, it is true that Gary and Samuel have an interesting mix of clients coming and going. And this is just a little insurance in case anything happens."

"You mean like T. J.'s attack today."

"No, of course not. You could have hurt him with that stuff."

Gwen shook her head. "Then just when *does* a person use it?"

"Well, you'll have to use your own good sense, Gwen. Hopefully, you'll never need it. It's just our way of saying welcome to the group."

Gwen stared at the little black cartridge. She didn't know what to say. The whole idea of needing to use pepper spray to defend herself from one of the law firm's clients was repulsive. "Thanks, Sharon."

"If you ever have to use it, just make sure it's pointing in the right direction. And then get out of the area as quickly as you can."

Gwen nodded. "Hopefully I will remember that if the need ever arises. Say, Sharon, do you know what the story with T. J. is? Is he Gary's client?"

"Well, he's been accused of rape and assault. But the woman accusing him is of disreputable character. We think she's just looking for a nice, fat settlement. But Gary will probably get T. J. off the hook. After all, the Washington Wolves are supposed to have a pretty good year ahead of them, and no one in the state really wants to see T. J. Thompson in trouble."

"But what if he really did something wrong?"

"Wrong? He probably just got a little rough with the girl. But she should be used to that sort of a thing since she is a prostitute and all."

Gwen didn't know how to respond. The more she heard, the more disgusting and sordid the whole thing seemed.

"You look shocked, Gwen. But then Candice explained how you've lived a very protected life. It might be hard to accept, but this is the real world. And it isn't always a pretty place. Folks like Candice and Gary are just trying to make it better."

Gwen wondered how defending dangerous criminals made the world any better. "I suppose I have led a sheltered life," she admitted. "But it was nice. I suppose I do need to change. It's just not easy."

"Change never is. But it's usually good for us."

"I suppose so. I remember how my dad used to say that what doesn't kill us will eventually make us stronger. But he was usually talking about my sister."

Sharon laughed. "Well, my dad used to say that only the strong survive."

Gwen frowned. Now, that was a scary thought. T. J. had seemed much stronger than she had this afternoon.

FIVE

Gwen found herself checking and rechecking the locks on her doors and windows during the weekend. Ordinary noises made her jump, and familiar shadows took on a sinister appearance. T. J. had invaded her safety zone, and her sense of security was shaken—even at home. She knew it was ridiculous and that T. J. had probably forgotten all about her by now, but somehow coming face-to-face with a person like that had drastically altered her safe little world.

It didn't help matters that she was living alone. It occurred to her now that when Aubrey left home for college, it was Gwen's very first time to live alone. She had gone straight from her parents' home to being David's wife, and even after David was gone, there had always been Aubrey. Now for the first time in her thirty-eight years she was utterly alone. And she didn't like it.

On Friday, she didn't sleep well. And the next day, she was reluctant to leave the house at all. She knew it was silly, but she was afraid she would simply go about clutching her pepper spray and constantly looking over her shoulder. The whole thing was embarrassing, and she felt like a fool. But worse than that, she felt like a prisoner—a prisoner of fear. And as much as she despised the confinement, she didn't know how to shake her frightened feelings off. At least she was able to force herself to go to church on Sunday, but she came straight home afterward.

Finally, Monday morning came, and she didn't know whether to be relieved or discouraged. But at least going to work would get her out of the house for the day. She was angry at herself for succumbing to this weakness, and decided if anything dreadful was going to happen, she might as well just face it head on and get it over with. Once again, she dressed carefully, hoping that today she would have a chance to discuss her job description with Candice. She certainly didn't expect Candice to make her a partner or anything like that, but she hoped that they could at least come to some sort of understanding. If Candice only wanted a moving person or an errand girl, then perhaps Gwen should look for another sort of job. But at least, at the end of the day, she could still be thankful for this brief experience. If nothing more, it had shown her that she could get out there and work.

As she drove to the office, she prayed. Not her usual prayer about working as if she were serving God, or even for an extra portion of strength. Instead she prayed that God would begin to divinely direct her life and give her a specific and a fulfilling purpose, as well as protect her.

She walked into the office with her head high, hoping to exude confidence that she did not completely feel. As she put away her purse and poured a cup of coffee, she heard Lucinda speaking very politely on the phone, as if the caller were very important and needed to be handled carefully.

"No, Mr. Black, Candice is not in yet. You'd like to come in at ten this morning? Let me check her schedule and see if that will work." Lucinda flipped through some pages. "Yes, ten o'clock looks just fine. I'll pencil you in. Thank you very much, sir." She hung up and made a note.

"Hi, Lucinda," said Gwen. "Was that Oliver Black?"

"Yeah, now I just hope Candice hasn't scheduled something else and not told me."

The phone rang again, and Lucinda turned back to her desk. Gwen went into the sample room to see if the carpenter had come during the weekend. Not only had he come, but he had completely removed two walls of shelves and left quite a mess behind as well. Gwen knew that Candice would flip to see her precious Persian carpet coated with sawdust. Hadn't the carpenter ever heard of drop cloths? She went to the cleaning closet and retrieved the vacuum and went right to work, hoping to finish before nine. She carefully vacuumed every bit of debris before there was any chance of grinding it into the nap of the jewel-toned carpet.

"Hello there," Sharon called from the hallway. "Cleaning up after the carpenter, I'll bet."

Gwen nodded. "Do they always leave messes like this?"

"Just Stanley. I don't know why Candice still uses him. But sometimes he's the only one available. Thanks for cleaning that up." She handed Gwen a slip of paper. "Candice left a message for you on my voicemail. There are some things she wants you to do this morning."

Gwen looked over the list. It was nothing too challenging, but a step up from moving things to the basement. "This sounds pretty straightforward," she said to Sharon. "Do you know when she's coming in?"

Sharon shook her head. "No. And I've got to get some bills ready to go before the mail gets picked up."

Gwen situated herself in the catalog room and began to work on her list, copying pages from catalogs, locating fabric samples, and ordering a few things. No big deal. It looked like Candice was getting some things ready to meet with a client. A light fixture that Candice wanted ordered was out of stock, and Gwen decided to check and see if Candice wanted her to locate something similar.

It was getting close to ten o'clock, perhaps Gwen could catch Candice before she met with Oliver Black. Gwen didn't really want to see Mr. Black today. She was still slightly embarrassed by their last encounter. He had been very nice and helpful, but she was afraid that she had come across as a little ditzy. And she really didn't like being cast in the weak, frightened, victim role.

She grabbed the light fixture catalog and slipped upstairs to Candice's office. But there was no sign of Candice. Had she even come in yet? What about the Oliver Black appointment? Gwen dashed back downstairs to check.

"Lucinda," said Gwen, "Is Candice in?"

Lucinda frowned. "Nope. And I haven't heard a word from her, either."

"So did you cancel—?"

Just then the door opened, and Gwen saw Lucinda grimace. "Uh, hello, Mr. Black," she said nervously.

Gwen turned around and forced a smile to her lips. "Good morning, Mr. Black."

"Good morning, ladies," he answered congenially.

Gwen quickly took in his appearance. He looked more casual today in corduroy pants with a tweed jacket over a denim shirt. It was a good look on him, making him seem younger somehow. And the blue denim seemed to bring out the blue in his eyes.

Gwen glanced at Lucinda who seemed to be at a total loss for words and decided to jump in to see if she could rescue this situation. She knew that Mr. Black had big potential and Candice had said to give him the VIP treatment.

"I understand that you scheduled an appointment for Candice at ten." Gwen looked at her watch and smiled. "And ten it is. But unfortunately Candice hasn't come in yet. And Lucinda hasn't heard a word from her. I hope she hasn't had an emergency." Gwen turned to Lucinda. "I'm sure you already tried to reach her at home as well as on her car phone."

Lucinda nodded and said hopefully, "I left a message on Candice's answering machine at home. Maybe she's on her way right now."

"Perhaps you'd like to a cup of coffee while you wait, Mr. Black," offered Gwen.

"That sounds good. I take it black." He followed her into the client meeting room.

"Lucinda, why don't you see if you can reach Candice on the car phone again," Gwen suggested as she went to get a cup of coffee.

"I will, Gwen. Thanks for your help."

Gwen returned with two cups of coffee. Oliver was comfortably seated in a club chair, and she handed him his cup and smiled. "I'm sorry about this inconvenience, Mr. Black. Lucinda is trying to reach Candice right now." She sat in the chair opposite him and took a sip of her coffee.

"It's probably my fault for not giving much notice," said Oliver apologetically, "but my morning was free, and the receptionist sounded as if it would be no problem."

"Well, hopefully Candice will come flying in here any minute."

"I hope so. I really wanted her to look at something this morning. I need to make a decision, and I don't have much time."

"I see," said Gwen. "Has Candice done other projects for you?"

"No, she was recommended by a friend. And actually I have several projects in mind, but the one I had planned to show her last week is getting to the critical stage where I need to make a move if I'm going to go through with it."

Gwen nodded. "Let me go see if Lucinda has had any luck."

"Thank you, Gwen," he said. "I really appreciate your help."

She was surprised that he actually remembered her name. She found Lucinda flipping through a magazine. "Did you reach her?"

Lucinda looked up. "Nope. I don't think she has her car phone turned on."

Gwen sighed. "Poor Mr. Black. This makes two times of being stood up."

Lucinda moaned. "So much for the VIP treatment, huh?"

"Shall I send him away?" asked Gwen.

"Maybe you could talk with him for a while," suggested Lucinda brightly. "Make it seem like a real consultation or something, you know, kind of fake it. I suppose you could write some stuff down for Candice while you're at it."

"Fake it?" said Gwen with raised brows. "Actually, I used to do this all the time. Maybe I could just spend enough time with him to salvage the relationship."

"That's the spirit, Gwen," said Lucinda. "Candice will really appreciate it."

Gwen went back in and tried to look confident. "Well, Mr. Black, I'm sorry, but Lucinda has been unable to reach Candice."

"I was afraid of that." His brows knit together in a thoughtful frown.

"However," began Gwen, hoping to sound more professional than she felt, "if you'd like, I would be more than happy to meet with you for a preconsultation, if it would be of any help."

He brightened. "Really? You'd do that?"

She nodded. "Of course."

"Okay then." He stood. "You'll have to come with me. I need a decorator to check out a piece of real estate that I want to make an offer on today. Will that work for you?"

"Sounds great. Let me get my purse."

She returned and followed him out to the parking lot. "Shall I follow you?" she asked.

"It might be easier if I take you, if you don't mind. Then I can explain what I need to know as we drive. Is that all right with you, Gwen?"

She felt a small wave of fear, a residue from her lousy weekend, but then reminded herself that this was a client, and according to Candice, a very important one. "It's fine, Mr. Black."

He opened the door of a sage green all-terrain vehicle. Gwen didn't know what make it was, but she was never one to pay attention to such things. But she could see by the comfy leather seats and wood-grained dash that it was very nice.

He buckled up his seat belt and turned to her. "One rule, though, could you please stop calling me Mr. Black. It makes me feel like an old man. Oliver is just fine."

She nodded. "Okay, Oliver. Now tell me about where you are taking me."

"Well, have you ever heard of the Alvadore Mansion?"

"I love that old place. Don't tell me you're buying it?"

"That's what I'm trying to decide today. I've had my eye on it for a while, and it just went on the market last week, and there are already several offers brewing. I wanted to make one last week. But I wanted an expert opinion first."

Suddenly Gwen wondered if she were totally out of her league. "Well, I don't know if I would call myself an expert, Oliver. I mean I've only worked on small projects in private homes and not for a couple of years. And I haven't really done much of anything yet for Candice. I don't want you to get the wrong impression—"

"Don't worry. It's not so much expertise as a good eye. Would you say you have a good eye?"

Gwen nodded. "Yes, I would say that. I just don't want to misrepresent myself."

"Thanks, I appreciate your honesty. If it makes you feel better, you can just pretend you are looking at a place with a friend."

"That sounds like fun. Now, tell me, what do you plan to do with the mansion?"

"Well, I've always thought it would make a pleasant place to stay—I thought perhaps a bed-and-breakfast. There really aren't any nice ones in town."

"Oh, that would be perfect. And it's so close to the park. And wouldn't it be a great place for weddings? I know my daughter used to say she wanted to be married up there."

"That's the daughter who's in college? Wasn't her name Aubrey?"

"Yes, that's amazing that you would remember."

"Well, it's an unusual name."

"I haven't been up here in ages," Gwen said as he turned up the road that led to the mansion.

"I would like to thin out some of these trees."

"Yes, it would brighten it up some. It can seem awfully gloomy up here sometimes. But you might have some problems with some of the preservationist crowds."

Oliver nodded. "That's true. Good thing to look into. Could you make a note of that?"

"Sure." Gwen pulled out a notepad. It was nice to feel useful. "You'll probably need to look into widening the driveway, too, and of course, you'll need parking. Unless you plan on having some sort of shuttle. Wouldn't a horse and carriage be sweet? I'm sorry, I'm getting carried away."

"Not at all. Please write down your ideas. This is exactly what I wanted."

"Is it open?" asked Gwen. "Can we go in?"

He held up a key. "The place is all ours."

"Isn't this porch wonderful?" exclaimed Gwen. "What a great place for guests to relax. You know even in cool weather a porch can be nice if you have some comfortable wicker furniture with nice cushions and throws and all."

"Are you writing all this down?" asked Oliver eagerly.

"You bet." Gwen quickly jotted down more notes.

"I know it needs a lot of work. Paint and carpentry repairs, a new furnace. But I think for the most part it's pretty solid. Even the roof is in good condition." He unlocked the oversized door, and they both walked in.

"The floors look to be in pretty decent shape," Gwen observed as they walked through a large front parlor. "Just a good refinishing should be enough." She looked at the carved wood trim that surrounded the doors, windows, and ceilings. "Isn't that beautiful?"

"Yes. Thankfully no one ever painted over it."

"That old varnish could probably be stripped and refinished to really bring out the beauty of that old wood."

"And look at this," Oliver said as he opened a set of double doors that led to a big solarium.

"Ahh," said Gwen, "this is where I would spend all my time."

"And if I thin those trees out it will be even lighter in here."

"What a pleasant place for guests to relax." Gwen examined the floor. "This floor looks shot, but ceramic tile or even a nice jute might be great in here."

"Make a note of that," said Oliver. "Let's see the rest of this place."

Gwen felt like a child at Christmas. Of course, this wasn't *her* house, or even her decorating assignment, but it was fun to participate. "Now, this kitchen will definitely need some work," she said as she looked at the big cast-iron sink and enormous old stove. "Your biggest expense will probably be in here, because if you plan to have breakfast served, everything will have to meet food preparation codes. Do you know anything about the plumbing and electrical?"

"The plumbing was all redone in the fifties. So the rough stuff should be fine, but we may want to update some of the bathroom fixtures. The electrical is old, but according to my real estate agent, it meets code."

"A lot of the light fixtures look original. I'm not sure what overall effect you're going for, but you might want to save them."

"I'd like to preserve a lot of the historical elements," said Oliver thoughtfully, "but at the same time I want it to be more relaxed and comfortable. I don't want a bunch of dark, old antiques and stiff chairs."

Gwen laughed. "Right. It sounds like you're going for a more casual look, but something complimentary to the house. Maybe sort of an English country style; friendly yet somewhat traditional. Of course, that would be between you and Candice. I'm just thinking out loud."

"I like how that sounds, Gwen. Don't forget to make a note of it."

They toured the second floor. The bedrooms looked as if they would need the least amount of work. Gwen suggested armoires in the rooms for extra storage space and to hold TVs and VCRs if needed. The third floor looked as if it had once been a ballroom.

"What will you do with this?" asked Gwen.

Oliver scratched his head. "I'm not sure."

"You could probably add more rooms," suggested Gwen. "Or perhaps divide it into a couple of luxury suites."

"That would be perfect," exclaimed Oliver. "Write that down." Then he turned to her. "Sorry, I don't mean to sound as if I'm ordering you around. I really appreciate you coming with me today. Candice is lucky to have you, Gwen. I was about ready to give up on her firm."

Gwen felt her cheeks glowing. It was the nicest thing anyone had said to her in weeks. Maybe months. "Thanks. I have really enjoyed this. It seems like a wonderful opportunity, Oliver. If the price is right, I don't see how you could go wrong in getting it. I assume you've already looked into the city codes as far as using it as a B-and-B."

"I've got my agent looking into all that, but he was fairly certain that it could be worked out. The city knows that it needs to develop more hospitality services. The other folks bidding on it are looking to do the same thing with it. I doubt that it will turn a profit for some time, what with all the fix-ups and outfitting, but that's a write-off in itself. I think in the long run it will prove a good investment. This property can only increase in value."

"I don't presume to know about all that, but I think it's a wonderful house with great potential."

He smiled. "Well, you've made my decision very easy, Gwen. I look forward to seeing what we can do with this place."

SIX

Candice didn't show up at work until midafternoon. Gwen had managed to complete the list that Sharon had given her and hoped to catch a few minutes of Candice's time to discuss her job, as well as to update her on the Oliver Black appointment.

"Hello, girls," Candice called as she breezed through. "Anything exciting going on today?"

"Where have you been?" asked Lucinda.

"I went to an auction this morning. Didn't I tell you about it last week?"

"Not that I remember," said Lucinda. "I thought you were coming in, and so I made an appointment with Oliver Black, but then you didn't show—"

"What?" exclaimed Candice. "Why didn't you check with me first, Lucinda? Good grief, that poor man is going to hate me."

"Well, thankfully, Gwen saved the day," said Lucinda proudly.

Candice turned to Gwen with a frown. "And how, may I ask, did Gwen save the day?"

"Well, Oliver had an urgent matter, so I offered to help him. And he asked me to go and look at it with him."

Candice blinked. "And did you go?"

"Sure. And it's a good thing—"

"Before you go any further, why don't you come up and explain all this to me in my office."

"Shall I get my notes?"

"Notes?" Candice asked with a puzzled look.

"Yes, Oliver asked me to take notes."

"Yes, I suppose I should look at them. And for future reference, Gwen, we don't call clients by their first names."

"I'm sorry, he asked me to call him Oliver."

Candice made a sound that sounded like a grunt. "Meet me upstairs, pronto!"

Gwen grabbed her notebook and followed Candice upstairs. "I was only trying to help," she explained as she sat down in the chair across from Candice's desk.

"I'm sure you were, Gwen. But you stepped over the line."

"The line?"

"Yes, the line. I am the designer here. You're the—the—actually, I'm not even sure what you are."

"I was hoping we could discuss that, Candice."

"Later. First let's discuss Oliver Black. Just what's he up to, anyway?"

"Well, Oliver—I mean, Mr. Black, said he has several projects he wants to discuss with you. But today he needed a consultation because he was trying to decide whether or not to place a bid for the Alvadore Mansion. He wants to turn it into a bed-and-breakfast."

"Interesting…" Candice folded her hands and leaned back in her chair.

"Yes, the place is wonderful. I went through the whole thing."

Candice frowned. "See, that's just what I mean. You had no business going through the house with him."

"But if I hadn't—"

"You stepped over the line, Gwen. And if you're going to work for me, you have to understand your boundaries."

Gwen felt like a five-year-old being scolded. And she'd only been trying to help. "Candice, I'm sorry that this upsets you. But the fact is, you weren't here. Oliver was ready to give up on you. If I hadn't gone with him, you would have lost this job for certain. And it looks like a great job, Candice. There are eight bedrooms and possibly two more—"

Candice cut her off. "You just don't get it, Gwen."

"Get what?"

"I didn't hire you to be a decorator."

"I know that." Gwen looked down at her hands. "I was just trying to rescue a—"

"I don't need rescuing."

"I thought you might want me to try and save Oliver as a client. Lucinda seemed to think it was the right thing to do."

"Lucinda doesn't run my design firm."

Gwen just stared at Candice in wonder. How could she be such a shrew about this whole thing? Gwen had only been trying to help. "Fine, Candice. Whatever. Do you want my notes or not? Maybe I should just pack up my things and go. We knew this might not work out from the beginning. I can see that it was probably not a good idea—"

Candice sighed. "Okay, okay. Wait a minute. Maybe I am getting a little carried away, Gwen. I'm sorry. But you do understand my point, don't you?"

"I suppose." Gwen studied Candice for a long moment.

"I know you have decorating experience, Gwen. But if you want to work for me, you will have to do things my way. You have a lot to learn, and if you're patient and work hard you might be able to work your way up—in time. No more taking my appointments with clients—understand?"

"If you say so. Now, do you want to go over my notes?"

"I suppose it wouldn't hurt."

Gwen described the house in detail, mentioning every

suggestion that Oliver had asked her to write down. She could see that Candice was making notes of her own, but it didn't appear that Candice cared much about Gwen's ideas. Oh, well, that was Candice's problem now. Gwen had tried. What more could she do?

"Is that it?" asked Candice impatiently.

"I think so. Do you want my notes?"

Candice laughed. "No thanks. I think I can handle it from here. On your way down, ask Lucinda to follow up with Mr. Black and see if we can schedule a consultation where I will actually be present. And tell her to double-check with me before she books anything."

"Okay. Before I go, I would like to have a better idea of exactly what my position is to be here, Candice."

Candice frowned. "I thought I already went over that."

"Well, you sort of—"

"It's too soon to really decide. I think I need to get a better idea of what you are capable of doing, Gwen. Is that too much to ask?"

Gwen shook her head. "I guess not."

"Now here's a list of some things I need done."

Gwen took the list. "Oh, yes, I almost forgot. Sharon had given me another list, and the light fixture you wanted ordered for the Grant's dining room is out of stock and won't be available until December. They have another one almost like it—"

"Well, get me a picture of it with the description so I can decide."

"I've got one downstairs. Also, I was wondering if I could have a desk someplace—maybe in the catalog room?"

"There's a desk in the basement you can use."

"Okay," said Gwen slowly. She stood up and moved toward the door. She hated the dark, musty basement but was tired of arguing with Candice. Maybe this job just was a big mistake. Maybe she should quit right now and save them both a lot of grief. But then again, what if this was her chance to really learn the trade? It had been such fun helping Oliver plan for his bed-and-breakfast. And she did hate to give up. She went downstairs and relayed Candice's message to Lucinda.

"Was Candice mad that you went with Mr. Black?" whispered Lucinda.

"She wasn't terribly pleased."

"I thought she'd be happy," said Lucinda, shaking her head. "But you can never tell with her."

Gwen sighed. "Now you tell me."

"Sorry."

Gwen went down to the basement and read over Candice's list. More samples to be gathered, several orders to be sent in, and a couple of errands in town. Well, maybe if she just kept proving herself in these little things, Candice would begin to trust her in the bigger things. Didn't the Bible say be faithful in small things and you might get bigger opportunities? Gwen looked around the dimly lit basement. Perhaps if she brought in some more light and maybe put some personal touches around, it could be a little more cheerful. Still she wasn't sure how long she could survive in this environment. It felt like she was being punished.

Just as Gwen was ready to go home, she met Candice in the parking lot.

"I've got an appointment scheduled with Oliver for Wednesday," said Candice.

"I'm surprised. I wouldn't think he'd know whether his offer had been accepted so soon."

"Apparently, it's not just the Alvadore Mansion," said Candice. "It sounds like he's got all kinds of things brewing. I'd really like to get on board with him. That guy has a lot of money."

Gwen pressed her lips together and nodded. "And he seems like a very nice person."

"Yes, and it would be helpful if you made sure you weren't around when I meet with him. You may have given him the impression that you are a designer, and I will need to make sure that he understands that he will be working with me. So keep a low profile on Wednesday morning, okay?"

"Sure. Good night, Candice." Gwen got in her car. She felt like crying but knew that was crazy. This was Candice's business, not hers. She had no right to feel shoved aside. She was lucky to have a job opportunity like this. If she could just swallow her pride and work hard, it might eventually grow into something better.

It was nice to be outside in the light again. Gwen rolled down her window and breathed in the cool September air. Before long it would be dark by the time she left the office. She couldn't imagine working all day in the dark basement and then coming out to darkness outside as well. But somehow she would manage. She had to.

At home, she turned on all the lights and even the TV, something she didn't usually do. She had always disliked it when her mother left her TV blaring all day, she said for the company, but now Gwen understood. She thought about how she had been plagued with fear all weekend over the T. J. incident last week. Somehow it all seemed rather ridiculous now, because she hadn't thought of him all day. At least *that* was something to be thankful for. Just the same, she checked the locks on the doors.

She ate cheese and crackers and an apple for dinner, then went to bed. As she lay in the darkness, she prayed. It was the way she had prayed after David had died. She asked God to hold her in his hand. She imagined resting there like tiny Thumbelina would have slept in a big human hand. And then she went to sleep.

The following day passed uneventfully. Candice had left a new list for her, longer than the previous ones. That was okay. She wanted to stay busy. She had brought a couple of lamps from home, a nicely matted and framed impressionist print to hang over her desk, and a few other things to brighten her basement workstation. And it helped. But by the end of the day she was eager to be outside. She stopped by the park on her way home to enjoy the late afternoon sunshine, even if only for a few minutes. It had been a while since she had taken a walk here. She tried not to look up at the Alvadore Mansion as she parked the car. She wanted to block out the pleasant time she had spent with Oliver. She knew that would be Candice's job. And if Gwen was lucky, she might get to order wallpaper or furnishings for the bedrooms.

"Hello there," called a masculine voice from behind.

She turned to see Oliver Black striding toward her with a friendly-looking black lab at his heels. "I thought that looked like you," he said as he approached.

"Hello," she answered in surprise. Oliver looked casual and comfortable in faded jeans and a tweedy gray sweater.

"This is Jasper," Oliver said as she bent down to scratch behind the big dog's floppy ears.

"Jasper," she said to the dog's face, "you are a real beauty."

"Don't be too nice or he'll follow you home."

Gwen stood and laughed. "That would be okay. In fact, I was thinking just this weekend that if I hadn't started working it would have been nice to have a dog around."

Oliver nodded. "You must be missing Aubrey."

It amazed her how he was so good at remembering names. "Yes. Actually, I was missing her a lot last weekend."

"Well, Jasper here is good company. And I'm not home all that much either during the day, but he manages to get along okay. Of course, Isobel is there."

Gwen nodded blankly. Isobel must be his wife. She tried to imagine what Oliver Black's wife might look like. Surely she would be beautiful. Maybe a blond, like Candice, but with a sweeter face and better disposition. Gwen stopped herself. "Yes, I've heard it's not good for animals to be alone too much."

"Or people," said Oliver.

Gwen felt her cheeks grow warm. "Yes, I'm sure you're right about that." She decided to change the subject. "I hear you have an appointment with Candice tomorrow."

He nodded. "Do you think she'll show?"

Gwen laughed. "I'm sure she will."

"I was just about to walk Jasper for a while. Do you want to join us?" asked Oliver.

Gwen considered how just a moment earlier she had been imagining his wife, but the fact was she didn't know for absolute certain that he was married. And even if he was, he was a nice person; it couldn't hurt to walk with him and his dog in a public place.

"Sure, that would be nice," she finally said. "I was wanting to take a walk, but I wasn't sure if—well, you know, since that incident with T. J. last week—" She stopped, unsure of what she even meant or wanted to say.

"I'm not surprised if you're fighting off the bogeyman in your mind," Oliver said as they began to walk down the trail toward the pond.

"Yes, that's exactly what it feels like. I keep telling myself that it's completely silly and a waste of time and energy, but it pops up just the same."

"Did you mention it to Candice?"

"Yes, but she didn't think there was anything to be concerned about. In fact, they all acted as if I were extremely paranoid."

Oliver nodded with a creased brow. "Well, let's hope she's right. Just the same, I wouldn't take any chances if I were you. Candice and the rest of them may have become a little jaded. But I remember reading in the papers about the accusation against T. J., and it sounded fairly serious."

"Well, they did equip me with pepper spray." She pulled her key chain from her pocket and grinned.

"I guess that's better than nothing." Oliver didn't look too convinced.

Gwen was on his left side, and as they walked she glanced quickly down at his left-hand ring finger. Nothing. But then again, she knew not every man who was married wore a ring.

"I've told you all about myself, Oliver—actually, Candice said I'm supposed to call you Mr. Black—"

"She did, did she?" Oliver chuckled. "Well, maybe that was for in the office."

"Maybe."

Oliver picked up a stick and gave it a good throw for Jasper. "You wanted to ask something about me?"

"No, not anything specific. Do you have any children?"

"Actually, I have two sons. Nathan and Nicholas. Nate is ten and Nick is twelve."

"Wow," said Gwen in surprise. "They must be a handful at that age."

Oliver nodded sadly. "Unfortunately, they are filling someone else's hands, most of the time anyway. I'm divorced and my ex has custody. I only see them every other weekend and some vacations and holidays."

"Oh, I'm sorry," said Gwen quietly. And she really was. She could hear the pain in his voice. How sad to be separated from your own children. It was hard enough having Aubrey living away. She couldn't imagine if she had lost her earlier.

"It's not quite as bad as that," said Oliver apologetically. "I go to their soccer games and school events, and we really have pretty good relationships despite everything."

"Yes, and I suppose it's not all that uncommon. It seems like at least half of Aubrey's friends have parents who were divorced. But still I think it's sad."

"I have to agree with you there. I think it's hard on the kids. But I try and be there for my boys."

"That's good. I'm sure they appreciate it."

Jasper came back again with the stick, this time dropping it at Gwen's feet. She picked it up and gave it a good chuck.

"Not bad," Oliver said with a grin.

"Thanks. Say, have you heard anything about the Alvadore place yet? Or is it too soon?"

"Well, my real estate agent sounded hopeful, but they have until tomorrow to respond to my offer. And there are other offers on the table."

"Can you raise your offer if it's rejected?"

"Yes, but I think I've offered a pretty fair price, and I hate to pay more than it's worth. It will take a lot to fix it up."

Gwen nodded. "You're probably right. It's a good thing I'm not involved in these kind of transactions. I'd probably let my emotions rule and wind up bankrupt in no time."

Oliver laughed. "Well, there's nothing wrong with having a heart when it comes to business, as long as you don't forget to use your head."

They stopped in front of the pond and Oliver gave Jasper's stick another good toss. The edge of the sky was turning orange and pink as the sun quickly slipped toward the horizon. And like a giant mirror, the pond was picking up the colors and reflecting them on the surface.

"That is incredibly beautiful," said Gwen. Just then Jasper dashed past them and leaped into the water.

"So much for the picturesque sight," laughed Oliver, then he whistled. "Come on back, Jasper. You know the park manager doesn't like dogs in his pond." Oliver looked over his shoulder as if expecting to be scolded. "Come on, Jasper!" Jasper finally turned around and paddled back to the edge and climbed out looking slightly sheepish.

"He does this every time," explained Oliver. "Labs are water dogs. You can hardly expect them to act—" Just then Jasper began to vigorously shake himself, drenching Gwen as he did.

"Jasper!" yelled Oliver, grabbing for his dog. "Stop it, you crazy mutt!" But it was useless trying to control him. Jasper was determined to shake off every drop.

Gwen was laughing now. "It's okay, Oliver." She looked down on her wet khaki pants. "Don't worry, these wash up just fine. Jasper didn't know what he was doing."

"I'm so sorry, Gwen. You'll probably think twice before you agree to go for a walk with us again."

"I've had a great time, Oliver. Really, don't worry about it." She leaned over and patted Jasper's damp head. "You didn't mean it, did you, Jasper? You were just trying to dry yourself off."

"Well, now I'll have to let Jasper run around to dry off completely, but we better get you back to your car before you freeze in those wet clothes."

They chatted pleasantly as they walked back across the

park. Gwen was sorry to say good-bye so soon, but Oliver was right, the cold autumn air was going right through her dampened pants. By the time they reached her car she was shivering.

"I'd like to take you out for a cup of coffee for the trouble we've caused you, but you would probably prefer to get dried off, so you must promise to let me make it up to you later. Okay?"

"You really don't need to—"

"Promise?"

"Sure, I'd like that."

Oliver smiled. "Good. Now, go get warm, Gwen."

She smiled and waved as she pulled out. Already she was feeling warmer. But it was coming from the inside. She turned on her car heater and drove home.

Maybe it hadn't been such a bad day after all.

SEVEN

Gwen purposely kept a low profile when Oliver came in to meet with Candice. No sense in rocking the boat. Besides she didn't want Candice to know that she and Oliver had gotten a little better acquainted yesterday. The fact was she felt slightly guilty about their unplanned meeting in the park but didn't know why. Their conversation really had nothing to do with Candice or the design firm, and even if it did, what difference should it make? Candice didn't own her. Gwen looked around the dark, dreary basement and suddenly felt very much like Cinderella. And the thought almost made her smile. Almost.

She turned back to the blue computer screen and tried to make sense of the on-line instructions Sharon had jotted down for her. Sharon had said it was so simple that even a child could do it, and Gwen was determined not to have to go back and ask for more help. She had several wall-covering orders to place that she would have rather placed by phone, but Sharon was adamant that Gwen learn how to do these tasks on-line and come into the twentieth century before the twenty-first began. Just as Gwen started to figure it out, the phone rang.

"Hello, this is Gwen Sullivan," she answered the phone just as she had been instructed to do.

"Hi, Mom."

"Aubrey! What a pleasant surprise. What's happening?"

"Oh, I was just thinking about you. You know you haven't called me for a while."

Gwen laughed. "Well, it seems I remember a certain daughter telling me not to call her so much."

"Yeah, but I didn't think you'd take me so seriously. It's been so long since I'd heard from you I got worried that you might have eloped with some wealthy businessman and left the country with no forwarding address."

"Well, actually I wasn't planning to do that until *next* weekend," teased Gwen.

"Then I'm glad I called. Do you suppose you could take some time out of your busy life to meet for lunch today?"

"I'd love to, Aubrey. Just say when and where."

It was quickly settled, and Gwen hung up and returned to her ordering. She wondered if something was wrong with Aubrey. Maybe she should have asked. But she would see her soon enough, and hopefully it was just a chance to catch up.

By the time Gwen placed the third order she could see that it really was quite simple. This modern-day technology was truly amazing. At noon, she went upstairs to get her purse. As she passed through a hallway she noticed Candice scowling darkly as she thumbed through her mail. Gwen wanted to ask how the appointment with Oliver had gone, but didn't want to sound too interested—or too nosy. Besides, she needed to be on her way to meet with Aubrey.

"You're certainly in a rush," Candice commented without looking up.

"Yes, I'm meeting Aubrey for lunch."

"Have fun," said Candice flatly.

"Thanks, I'm sure we will." As Gwen started her car she wondered if Candice ever regretted her decision not to have children. Whenever the topic came up, Candice always brushed it off saying her life was too full and busy for children, but sometimes Gwen wondered. Of course, it wasn't too late.

Candice was the same age as Gwen, and it wasn't all that unusual for women to have babies at their age, but the thought of Candice and Gary raising a child was somewhat unsettling. Candice had always seemed a little self-absorbed to Gwen— not exactly the warm, nurturing type. But then Gwen wondered if Candice had had children, perhaps that would have changed. Or perhaps Candice had made the right choice after all. Well, whatever, Gwen was certainly thankful for her daughter.

"Hi, honey," Gwen said as she spotted Aubrey's straight back, waiting at the busy café. Aubrey turned and hugged her.

"Mom!" she cried. "It's so good to see you!"

"Is everything okay, Aubrey?" asked Gwen with concern.

"Yes, everything's fine. I just missed you is all. And I think I got a little homesick."

"Really?" said Gwen with sympathy. "Why didn't you call or come over? I was missing you too."

"I wanted to be strong, Mom." Aubrey held her chin up in the same way she had when she was only four and saying, "I can do it myself, Mommy."

"You are strong, Aubrey. I wish I were as strong as you are."

"Oh, Mom, you're one of the strongest people I know."

Gwen looked at Aubrey in surprise. But before she could respond they were being shown to a table by the window and hearing the day's specials. They quickly placed their orders and resumed their conversation.

"I want you to tell me absolutely everything that's been happening at your new job," said Aubrey.

"Actually, it's been pretty uneventful—except for a couple of odd things that aren't really work related."

"Odd things?"

Gwen told Aubrey about her encounter with T. J., trying to make it sound like nothing and joking about the pepper spray that was given to her. She didn't want Aubrey to know how frightened she had been.

"That's horrible, Mom. You should watch out for that guy. He sounds like bad news to me."

"I suppose he could be." Gwen glanced out the window and continued in a low, almost mysterious voice. "And then I met a rather interesting man...."

"And?" Aubrey's eyes were wide with interest.

"Well, there's not really much to tell. He just seems like a nice person."

"Mom!" Aubrey's exasperation was plain to see. "You can't just casually mention something like *that* and then give no details. Tell me everything."

So Gwen launched into the story of how Oliver had come into the office at just the right moment to rescue her from T. J., and then how she had later gone to look at the Alvadore Mansion with him, and finally their meeting just yesterday in the park with his dog.

"Wow, Mom, that does sound intriguing. So when do you think he'll take you out for coffee?"

"I don't know..." Gwen twisted the napkin in her lap. "Maybe he was just being nice. He might not really want—"

"Well, I don't know why not, Mom. You are an intelligent and attractive woman. And if this Oliver Black is smart, he ought to know a good thing when he sees it."

Gwen laughed. "You make it sound as if I'm on the auction block: going once, going twice, sold to the smart man in the gray flannel suit."

Aubrey smiled. "I didn't mean it like that."

"I know. It's just that this whole idea of meeting a man and possibly going out for coffee or anything like that is completely foreign to me. Frankly, I don't like the idea of dating at all."

"But do you want to remain single?"

Gwen thought about that for a long moment. "Oh, I don't know for sure, Aubrey. Do you realize it's the first time in my life that I have actually lived alone? And while it has been rather lonely and I've even gotten scared—especially with that T. J. business—it is sort of nice to be my own woman, so to speak."

Aubrey nodded. "Nothing wrong with that, Mom. I think it would be awful if you thought you had to have a man. Jessica Wilson's mom is like that. She's in her fourth marriage right now, and I think it's disgusting."

"Well, I can't speak for Jessica's mom, but I would rather be single than go through that. Good relationships take a lot of work. I know I couldn't just hop in and out. I guess that's what worries me. I don't want to have to go out looking. I just don't think I can play the dating game."

Aubrey laughed. "Now, that's where you and I are different. I think it's fun to meet lots of new people. The more the merrier."

Gwen nodded enthusiastically. "Yes, and I think that's exactly right for you, Aubrey. You're young, and you should have lots of friendships with both guys and girls. And hopefully you're not looking for a serious relationship yet."

"No way. I've got too much to do before I settle down."

"But for me, getting involved with a man feels more serious. After seventeen years of a good marriage with your dad, it's hard for me to imagine casually dating a variety of men. And getting involved at all is rather frightening. Does that make any sense?"

"Sure it does, Mom. I admire that about you. And I always remember what you told me last year."

"What's that?" Gwen sipped her tea and studied her daughter's face. Sometimes, like now when Aubrey was being serious, she looked so much like her father that it was almost hard to look at her without choking up.

"Mom, do you remember when I asked you last Christmas if you ever thought you'd marry again?"

Gwen nodded slowly. It was one of those moments she would always remember.

"Well, you said that if God had someone special for you, then he would have to bring him into your life and make it very obvious because you had no intention of going out to look for someone."

Gwen smiled. "That's right. And I still feel that way."

"Well, could it be possible that this Oliver Black might have been brought into your life for a reason?"

Gwen sighed. "I suppose it's possible. But it is equally possible that he was not. I guess all I can do is wait and see."

Aubrey smiled. "That's right. And you better keep me informed. I don't want to read in the paper that you ran off to marry some stranger."

Gwen laughed and looked at her watch. "Speaking of running, I better get back to work. And I promise to keep you informed. And remember it works both ways. You can call or come by anytime you like."

They hugged and parted ways. Gwen was so thankful for Aubrey. And it seemed her mother's advice had been right. It reminded Gwen of the old nursery rhyme, "Leave them alone and they'll come home, wagging their tails behind them."

"It's about time you were back," Candice said in a grumpy tone as soon as Gwen walked in the door.

"It's barely past one," said Gwen defensively. Then she smiled. "Sorry, Candice. Do you need me to do something?"

"Yes, I want you to come on a job with me. We need to do

lots of measuring. Are you ready?"

"Sure, just let me grab a notebook and a tape measure."

They rode in Candice's Jaguar. Candice zipped in and out of traffic as if she were driving the Indy 500.

"I hope I didn't make you late," Gwen said as she watched them approach the back end of a pickup too fast.

Candice laughed. "Does my driving scare you, Gwen? I always drive like this. I figure it's safer to drive offensively than defensively."

Gwen swallowed and nodded. "I see."

"Well, don't you want to know how my meeting with Mr. Black went today?" asked Candice.

"Sure. How did it go?"

"Rotten."

Gwen turned and stared at Candice. Was she joking? "Rotten?"

"Yes. I have absolutely no intention of taking *that* job. And I think he has a lot of nerve to even ask me."

Gwen didn't know what to say. How could Candice turn down Oliver Black? And what about the Alvadore Mansion? It would be a decorator's dream. "Are you sure about this, Candice?" asked Gwen meekly.

Candice laughed. "Absolutely certain. I told Gary about it at lunch, and he thinks that Oliver Black is nuts. He doesn't want me to work for him *ever.*"

"I just don't understand—"

"Well, here we are," Candice announced as she pulled into a parking lot of one of the larger office buildings in town. She quickly described what they would be doing as they walked in. It sounded like a big job. Gwen tried to push away their earlier conversation about Oliver and to concentrate on the tasks that

Candice was throwing her way. This was her chance to show Candice what she was capable of, and it would take her full concentration to do so.

Gwen measured and wrote again and again, following Candice around like a robot. She didn't even have time to think about the look that Candice was going for or what style of decor Candice would choose. She only had time to measure and write as they moved from room to room.

After several hours, they were finished and back in the car. Gwen's head felt as if it were spinning with numbers and measurements still flying all around. She had never measured so many windows, walls, and floors in her life.

"That went lots faster than I expected," Candice said as she roared out of the parking lot. "I didn't think we'd actually be able to finish it today."

Gwen wondered if that was a compliment, but decided to say nothing. Instead she leaned back and tried to relax, hoping that Candice's offensive driving theory really did work. She wanted to question Candice further about Oliver Black but couldn't quite think of where to start. It still dumbfounded Gwen to think that Candice would throw away a job like that.

As if reading her mind, Candice began to speak. "Yes, that Oliver Black is quite a guy. Just because he's one of the richest people in town, he thinks that I would want to work for him. Well, I haven't told him my decision yet, but I wish I could see his face when I turn him down. Of course, I will have to tell him by phone."

"But it seemed like a great opportunity, Candice…"

"Ha! That's what you think. Well, it's about time you learned, Gwen dear, that in the business world people aren't always what they seem. They show you what they think you want to see, and then—boom—they switch gears without even warning you. My meeting with that man was a complete waste of time today. And I would rather not speak about it. The fact is, Oliver Black is a big jerk!"

Gwen turned and looked out the passenger window. It hurt to hear Candice speak like that about Oliver. But it was even more troubling to try to figure out why. What could he have possibly done to have set Candice off like this? And Gary too? It just made no sense. Especially if Oliver was as well-off as Candice had insinuated. Gwen knew from experience that Candice had great respect for wealth. None of this added up. But Gwen didn't want to press Candice for further explanation right now. Maybe later when she didn't seem so aggravated about the whole thing.

It was quitting time when they reached the office. Gwen thankfully got out of Candice's car. Maybe next time she would offer to drive or meet Candice.

"Thanks for your help, Gwen," Candice said in an almost cheerful voice.

Gwen blinked. "Sure. Thanks for letting me tag along. See you tomorrow."

Gwen felt confused as she drove toward home. She considered stopping at the park, but was afraid she might bump into Oliver. And then what would she say? He must have said or done something pretty bad to have turned Candice against him like that. But Gwen couldn't imagine what. He seemed like such a nice person. She remembered how thoughtful he had been at the park when Jasper had gotten her all wet. Now she wondered if she would ever get the chance to know him better. Once Oliver learned that Candice was turning him down, he might not want to spend any time with Gwen, either. And of course there was the possibility that Oliver was not the person she thought he was. She felt like a dog chasing its tail—she was getting nowhere with her fretting.

"Just forget about it for now," she said out loud. Then she remembered the verse about casting all her cares on God because he cared for her. And that's what she did.

When she got home, she noticed the red light blinking on her answering machine. Probably her mother, she hadn't heard from her for a while. Gwen pushed the play button and slipped off her shoes.

"Hello, Gwen," said a masculine voice. "This is Oliver Black. I wanted to see if you remembered your promise to let me take you out for a cup of coffee. Well, actually, I was hoping that I could upgrade from coffee to dinner. But I don't want to be too pushy. Why don't you give me a call?"

Gwen wrote down the phone number and stopped the machine. Then she rewound the message and listened to it again. She liked the sound of his voice. It was deep and strong sounding, yet warm and kind. He seemed so nice. What could he possibly have done? Maybe she should ask him right up front. But then again that seemed so rude.

She wished she had someone to talk to about this. She remembered how interested Aubrey had been in hearing everything about Oliver Black. But it was almost six, Aubrey was probably at dinner by now. Gwen dialed her number anyway and was surprised to hear her daughter answer.

"Hi, Aubrey," she said in an apologetic tone. "I thought you might have already gone to dinner."

"No, I was just about to go."

"Well, I know we just talked, and if you need to go, I'll understand. But I wanted to run something by you if you have a minute."

"Sure, Mom. What's up?"

"Well, remember what I told you about Oliver Black?"

"Yeah, don't tell me he's popped the question."

Gwen laughed and then quickly told Aubrey about what Candice had said, then about the message on her answering machine. "What should I do, honey?"

"Wow, Mom. That's a toughie. On one hand, I really liked the sound of this Oliver guy. But if Candice has a problem with him I'd say that's a big warning sign. I mean, Candice thinks T. J. is okay, so we know her standards aren't too high anyway. And you say that even Gary didn't want Candice to work with Oliver?"

"That's what she said. It just doesn't make sense."

"No. And seems I remember a certain mom always telling me, 'When in doubt, don't.'"

"Yes, that same thought went through my mind." Gwen sighed. "It's just that he seemed so nice…"

"Is there some way you can check up on him?"

"I don't want to bring it up with Candice again. Hey, I've got an idea. Mary Powers."

"Who's that?"

"A woman I met through Candice. She's a real-estate agent and her husband is in investments. They seem like the type of people who might know someone like Oliver. Plus, I promised to take Mary to lunch. She was the one who nudged Candice to get me this job."

"And you're still thinking that's a good thing?"

Gwen laughed. "Well, it has its moments. Thanks for listening, Aubrey. I'll call Mary and see if she knows anything about Oliver. Now you better get down there for dinner before it's too late."

"Okay, Mom. Thanks for calling. Let me know how the continuing saga of Oliver Black unfolds."

Gwen hung up and went into the kitchen. Tonight she was

determined to fix something more than just canned soup. She dug around in the freezer until she found a package of frozen ravioli and some broccoli. She boiled the ravioli and heated some tomato sauce. She even grated some Parmesan cheese. Then she arranged this on a plate and sat down at the breakfast bar to eat. It seemed a small thing, but to her it was a major victory.

She waited until after seven to call Mary. First she reminded Mary of the promised lunch date if Gwen's job worked out with Candice, and then they chatted about how Mary's house was coming along.

"I know Candice is working as fast as she can, but it sure doesn't look like we'll be in by Thanksgiving, Gwen."

"Hmm. I wonder if there's anything I can do to help. I'll check with Candice tomorrow."

"Oh, that would be great. I know these things take time. But we had really hoped to get settled. Now where shall we meet for lunch, Gwen?"

"How about Giovanni's at noon?"

"Sounds great. I'm so glad you called, Gwen. I've been thinking about you and wondering how you're doing."

"Well, we can get all caught up tomorrow," said Gwen. She had decided to bring up Oliver at lunch. Then she could make it sound like a more casual question. And maybe she'd finally get some answers.

EIGHT

G wen met Mary at Giovanni's. Mary looked every bit the successful business woman in her cream gabardine suit.

"It's so nice to see you again," said Mary. "You look gorgeous, Gwen. And I love what you've done with your hair."

"Thanks. It was my daughter's idea. But I like it, too."

"It looks like our table's ready," Mary said as she headed across the restaurant. Gwen followed. She admired Mary's style. It was different than the way Candice came across. Mary exuded confidence, and yet she seemed to really care about others. It was a sort of a gentle confidence.

"I spoke to Candice about your house," Gwen said as the waiter filled their water glasses. "I asked if I could help her keep tabs on orders and whatnot to try to keep it on schedule. And Candice seemed relieved to let me do it."

"Oh, bless you, Gwen. Ray will be relieved to hear that. We both think Candice is wonderful, but sometimes she spreads herself a little too thin. That's why we were both so glad to see her take you on. So tell me, how's it going?"

"Well, it's had its ups and downs. But I think it's going to be fine. I have so much to learn still, and I know I have to pay my dues, so to speak. And, of course, this is a great opportunity for me."

Mary nodded. "It must be hard. But I bet you're going to be a big success, Gwen. I just get a feeling about people sometimes, and that's how I felt the moment I met you."

Gwen smiled. "Thanks, Mary. Right now I'll take all the encouragement I can get."

The waiter returned to take their order. Gwen ordered the pasta of the day, and Mary ordered the same.

"So," continued Mary after the waiter left. "Have you had a chance to do anything that's even slightly fun at work yet?"

"Actually, I had a delightful time going through the Alvadore Mansion just last week. That place is amazing."

"Oh, how exciting! I so wanted to place an offer on it, but Ray absolutely put his foot down. Still I think it would have been a good investment. So then, you must know who is buying it. Of course, you don't have to tell me if you don't want to, but I'm dying to know."

"Actually, I don't know if his offer has been accepted yet. But I can't see that there's any harm in saying who took me through the mansion. Do you know Oliver Black?"

"Of course. Well, I don't know him really well. But Ray does. And goodness knows, that man can certainly afford it. Do you know what he plans to do with it?"

Gwen wondered if she was saying too much, but then Oliver had not appeared concerned about keeping anything quiet. And if Candice knew about something, it was only a matter of time until everyone in town knew. "I think he wants to turn it into a bed-and-breakfast. It would be a perfect location, within walking distance to town and right next to the park."

"That would be nice. Well, I hope he gets it. Will Candice do the decorating then?"

Gwen frowned. "No, I don't think so."

"Why in the world not?"

"I'm not really sure. But I know that Candice plans to turn him down, and in fact, she may have already. I think it's a shame. It would be such fun to do."

"I can't imagine why Candice would turn him down. Unless she's too busy. Still it's such a great opportunity, I'd think she would make the time. And with you there to help. Well, it's a shame, Gwen."

"I know. And I really liked Oliver Black."

Mary's brows raised. "That's right, he's single, isn't he?"

Gwen nodded. "And he has asked me to dinner."

Mary grinned. "Well, just because Candice has turned him down doesn't mean you need to."

"I know. But Candice was so strange about the whole thing, she almost made it seem like there was something seriously wrong with him. She said that Gary didn't want her working for him."

"That's odd." Mary looked clearly puzzled.

"I know. It puts me in an awkward position. I'd like to go out with him, but after Candice carried on like that I feel a little uncertain. My instincts say he's okay, but then my instincts haven't had any practice for ages. This whole dating thing is completely new to me."

"Hmm…" Mary looked thoughtful as the waiter set their entrees on the table. "Maybe I could check up on him for you. Like I said, Ray knows him pretty well. Not only that, but I have a woman friend who is still very close to Oliver's ex-wife. Do you want me to do some sniffing around?"

"I hate to be snoopy, but after Candice's response it would be nice to know a little more about him before I get involved. It's hard making a big step like this, and like I said, I'm not too sure about my own instincts. If you wouldn't mind, Mary, I'd really appreciate hearing what Ray has to say."

"I don't mind a bit. And I think in this day and age one can't be too careful when it comes to dating."

Gwen smiled. "Yes, my daughter Aubrey said almost the same thing last night."

Mary smiled. "It's funny when your children start giving you advice, isn't it?"

"Yes, especially when you can hear yourself in their words. Do you and Ray have children?"

"Yes, we've got two grown sons. One's in med school, and the other's in the air force."

"So you know all about empty-nest syndrome."

Mary smiled. "Yes, I went through quite a time a couple years back. I thought because I was working it wouldn't be so bad. But when my baby, Justin, joined the air force, I just about fell apart. It's one thing having them go off to college, but the military— well, let's just put it this way: I have become a praying mother."

Gwen nodded. "It's so hard to let them go. I guess praying is about all we can do sometimes."

It was a pleasant lunch and what felt like the beginning of a good friendship. Mary winked at Gwen as they parted on the sidewalk outside Giovanni's. "I'll call and let you know what I find out," she promised.

Gwen spent the afternoon zipping around town doing errands for Candice. She didn't really mind. It was nice getting out of the basement, and it was fun to familiarize herself with the local businesses that Candice utilized for various design elements. She was particularly interested in the lamp-shade lady, Delores Harding. This woman worked out of her home creating beautiful one-of-a-kind lamp shades by cutting designs that allowed the light to come through. They really were works of art, and Gwen decided to order one for herself. She told Delores how much she liked light and how she never seemed to get enough of it.

"I know just what you mean," said Delores. "I used to wonder why I even stayed in the Northwest. It can get so dark and dreary around here in the winter. But then I realized that the gloominess makes me appreciate the light so much more. You know it makes a nice contrast—sort of like my shades. And of course, I imagine that folks appreciate my shades even more up here, too, since we're such a light-deprived people."

"That makes sense," said Gwen. "I guess I never looked at it like that."

Gwen thought about what Delores had said as she drove back to the office. That building seemed like such a light-deprived place to her. Not just physically, but spiritually as well. Perhaps God had placed Gwen there so she could be a light for Candice and Sharon and Lucinda. A contrast to the darkness. Well, Gwen could try her best. But she knew that God would have to shine through her.

She unloaded the back of her car and carried several items down to the basement. She stopped to check her messages on her phone and was surprised to hear Oliver's voice again. She had meant to call him sometime today, to at least let him know she had gotten his earlier message, but she had been uncertain about how to answer his invitation. But today's message was suggesting that perhaps it would be better for them to meet for coffee. She wondered if he had been having second thoughts about her, too. Well, having coffee didn't seem like too big of a deal. She picked up the phone and dialed the number he had left. She knew he was a busy man and expected to get either his voice mail or his secretary. But it was Oliver who answered.

"Hi, this is Gwen," she said nervously.

"Hi Gwen. So how about it, can I meet you at Starbucks for a cup of coffee after work?"

"Sure. That sounds good. I was planning on leaving in about twenty minutes."

"Okay, I'll meet you there."

Gwen hung up and thought for a moment. Was this a mistake? She didn't think so. But she wasn't certain, either. Suddenly she remembered what Mary had said about praying for their kids. Well, Gwen was certain that God loved her even more than she loved Aubrey, and in that same moment she asked him to lead and guide her.

She finished putting things away in the basement and closed up her work station. On her way out, she stopped by the bathroom to check her appearance. She ran her fingers through her hair and applied some fresh lipstick, then critically studied her reflection. It was strange to care about her appearance like this. She had never considered herself to be particularly vain, but suddenly her looks mattered. She chided herself for acting like a high school girl and turned away. They were only meeting for coffee. Nothing more. This would be a chance for her to attempt to figure out exactly who Oliver Black really was. She was certain that he would have heard from Candice by now in regard to her refusal to work with him. Surely that would provide a topic of conversation that could prove to be very revealing.

She reached Starbucks before Oliver and went ahead and ordered a cappuccino and seated herself at a tall table by the window. She watched as people came and went, but Oliver didn't come. Just as she was about to decide that she had been stood up, he walked in. He rushed over to her and began to apologize.

"I had taken Jasper to the park—I thought he could run around for twenty minutes while I waited for you to get off work. And the crazy dog took off after a Dalmatian and I had to chase him."

Gwen laughed. "And then did he jump into the pond, too?"

Oliver grinned. "No, thank goodness. He's safe and dry and in the back of my Jeep." He looked at her empty cup. "I see you went ahead without me—not that I can blame you. But can I get you another cup?"

She looked at his flushed cheeks and disheveled hair and smiled. "Sure. But make it a decaf cappuccino this time."

He returned with two steaming cups and sat down. "I'm glad you didn't give up on me."

"Well, it was getting close." She took a sip.

"So did you hear the news?"

She stared at him for a moment. Did he mean about Candice. "I'm not sure," she began. "What news?"

"My offer was accepted. I got the Alvadore Mansion."

She smiled. "That is really great, Oliver. Congratulations. You must be very happy."

"I am. There's just something about that place. I mean, it's a good investment and all, but it's really more than that. I just found out yesterday. That's why I had called and asked about dinner. I wanted to celebrate, and since you had been kind enough to look at the place with me, I thought you would enjoy a celebration."

"I'm sorry. I meant to call today, and it got busy—"

"No problem. I understand. Besides, the agreement had been for coffee. And then I almost stood you up at that. So how is work going for you?"

"All right."

"I finally met with Candice yesterday."

"Yes, so I heard."

"She didn't seem terribly eager about my little project."

Gwen nodded. "No, she didn't." An understatement.

"She was supposed to call me today to let me know her decision."

"And she didn't?"

"No. I guess I won't be surprised if she doesn't want to take me on." Oliver sighed and took a sip of his coffee.

"Really?" Gwen asked as she carefully studied his face. "Why not?"

"It's not really her sort of project. The only reason I came to her was because of a mutual friend, Ray Powers. Apparently she is doing his house and Ray thought she was pretty good."

"I know Ray and Mary," said Gwen. "Actually I know Mary better than Ray. But I like them both."

"They're good folks."

"But I don't understand why you don't think it would be Candice's sort of project," said Gwen.

Oliver shrugged. "Oh, I don't know. She's more of an uptown sort of designer—very much into a traditional style. I think it was probably just a mismatch. Although I would have liked to have had you work on the project. You seem to have a good sense of decor, and I liked your ideas for the bed-and-breakfast."

Gwen smiled. "Thanks. I would have loved to have helped on that. I was really disappointed when I heard Candice was turning you down."

"Aha," said Oliver. "So she is turning me down."

Gwen's hand flew to her mouth. "Oops, sorry. I guess I shouldn't have said that."

"No problem. But it would have been nice if she had let me know herself. It's a funny way to do business, if you ask me."

Gwen didn't know what to say.

"But I didn't invite you to meet me for coffee so we could discuss Candice's business ethics," said Oliver.

"So, when do you expect to start renovations on the Alvadore place?"

"Oh, probably not for a while yet. I've got someone looking into all the codes and historical preservation things. I don't want to step on any toes."

Gwen nodded. "That sounds like a smart way to proceed." But she wondered if he wasn't in a hurry to begin renovating, then why had he been so eager to meet with Candice? Of course, there was some other project too. Still, she was determined not to bring Candice back into the conversation.

"I will probably try to get someone working on the larger repairs before winter sets in. I hate to see the place get any worse than it already is. But as far as any designer decisions—I can wait. I've got enough other projects to keep me busy in the meantime. But I hope to get something started in there by the new year."

They chatted together congenially for almost an hour. Then Oliver looked at his watch. "I hate to leave Jasper in the Jeep for too long."

"Yes, it is getting late." Gwen started to stand.

"Thank you for meeting me. And again, I apologize for being late."

"No problem. Thanks for asking me. I usually just rush home after work. It's nice to do something different for a change."

"So, would you mind if I called you again sometime?"

Gwen paused for a brief moment. She still didn't know all that much about him. But she liked what she knew. "Sure, that would be fine, Oliver. Tell Jasper hello for me."

Oliver grinned. "Will do. Maybe you'll be brave enough to take a walk with us in the park again."

"Sure. I'll just know to keep a safe distance when Jasper plunges into the pond."

"See you around, Gwen."

Gwen drove home with a smile on her face. She didn't know what Candice's problem with Oliver could be, but she couldn't imagine that it was anything worth worrying about. Gwen felt perfectly comfortable with him and she was looking forward to getting to know him better.

NINE

The next morning Gwen found Lucinda sitting at her desk with her head in her hands and tears flowing freely. No one else was around, and although Gwen normally tried to remain unobtrusive, she knew she couldn't ignore this.

"What's wrong, Lucinda?"

Lucinda sniffed. "Nothing really."

Gwen gently patted Lucinda on the back. "Well, if there's anything I can do, please let me know. Okay?"

Lucinda looked up with watery eyes. "Really?"

"Of course." Gwen smiled. "I wouldn't offer to help if I didn't mean it."

Lucinda wiped her nose on a tissue. "Well, some people offer to help just so they'll sound nice. So I never know for sure."

"Well, I mean it, Lucinda. Is there something you need to talk about?"

Lucinda took a choppy breath. "Well, it's just so hard sometimes. I mean working full-time and raising a child all on my own...."

Gwen slowly shook her head. "That must be really hard. Do you have anyone to help out with your little girl—I don't think I know her name?"

"Sierra. She's almost two, and as much as I love her, she can be a real handful sometimes. When I pick her up from day care all I want to do is go home and rest, but Sierra is all hyped up and wants my attention, and I get all grumpy and then—" Lucinda burst into fresh tears.

"And then you probably aren't as patient as you would like to be?"

Lucinda nodded. "And I'm afraid that Sierra is going to grow up to hate me."

Gwen put her hand on Lucinda's shoulder. "I don't think so, Lucinda. But it does sound as if you could use a hand. Do you have a mom or any family nearby who could help out?"

"My mom lives in California, and besides, she is completely hopeless. And I don't have any family around here."

"That must be really tough." Gwen thought for a moment. "Do you ever get time to yourself, to relax or just do something you enjoy?"

Lucinda sadly shook her head. "I can't even afford a baby-sitter. Right now, I can barely make ends meet. Candice and Gary have all these big ideas about me making it in the working world, but I don't think they know how hard it is. Sometimes I just want to give up and go on welfare or something. That's what a lot of single moms like me would have to do, you know."

"I can understand how you could feel like that, Lucinda. But in the long run you'd probably be sorry if you gave up. I have an idea, though. How about if I watch Sierra for you once in a while so that you can have some time on your own? I love little kids, and I'm at a place in life where I could use something extra to keep me busy."

"Really? You'd really baby-sit Sierra for me? For free?"

Gwen nodded. "I'd love to, Lucinda. Maybe we could start with one evening a week. Or maybe Saturday mornings. Or both. Whatever works best for you."

Lucinda's face brightened. "I think you'd really like Sierra,

Gwen. She's a bright little girl, and she can talk up a storm. But she's constantly on the go."

"That sounds pretty normal for an almost-two-year-old. You wouldn't want her to be any other way."

"I guess so. But sometimes I just feel so tired."

"Well, I think it's because you need a break. And I'd love to help you to get one. So, for starters, should we plan on Saturday morning? Do you want me to pick her up or would it be better for you to drop her by?"

"I can drop her by. Then I can see where you live."

"Okay, it's settled then."

"Thanks, Gwen. I feel better already."

"Thank you, Lucinda. It will be a pleasure getting to know your daughter."

Gwen went happily down to the basement and turned on the lights. She also turned on an air filtration device that she had brought in to help clean the musty air. It seemed to help a little, but she was still a bit concerned that breathing this stale air wasn't very healthy. She wanted to ask Candice about the possibility of moving her office upstairs but was waiting for the right moment. And perhaps as she became busier helping Candice, she would spend less time down here anyway. She finished up ordering some fabrics and went upstairs to get a cup of coffee.

"Hello there, Gwen," said a man's voice from behind her. She turned to see T. J. coming through the back door.

"Hello," she answered stiffly.

"You're looking real good, Gwen," T. J. said with a smile she did not like.

"T. J., why are you using the back door?" she asked bluntly, hoping to sidetrack him.

He laughed sarcastically. "Is that a problem for you?"

"Well, clients usually enter through the front door."

"Well, maybe I'm special, Gwen." He stepped up to her and looked in her face. "Do you think I'm special?" He was too close, but Gwen didn't move.

She felt flustered but was determined to stand her ground. She didn't want him to think she was weak. She squared her shoulders and said, "I happen to think that everyone is special, T. J. But I also think clients would be better served if they used the front door. And I would suggest that you come in that way."

T. J. narrowed his eyes and turned away without answering, sauntering on up toward the reception area. She hoped he had gotten her message, but she doubted it. Regardless of what Candice and the others thought, she still didn't trust him a bit.

"Hey, my man!" Gary said loudly from the reception area. He gave T. J. a high-five and a big pat on the back. "How're you doing, T. J.?"

"All right," T. J. answered, looking over his shoulder to where Gwen was still standing in the shadows in the hallway. "But I just got read the riot act for coming through the back door. Geez, I didn't know you folks had all these rules about which door to use."

Gary frowned in Gwen's direction. "We don't have rules, T. J. You can use any door you like. *Someone* must have gotten a little confused."

T. J. laughed. "Well, you know how those pretty heads are usually full of fluff. She probably can't help it."

Gwen took in a deep breath and turned on her heel. She could hear them both laughing and joking, probably at her expense, as she went down the stairs to the basement. What a horrible place to work, she thought as she sat down at her desk and looked around the dreary basement. What a spiritually dark environment. Suddenly she remembered her prayer about being a light here. Well, it shouldn't be too hard to be a light in this dark place. But on the other hand, it sure wasn't easy, either.

Just before noon, Gwen's phone buzzed. She picked it up to hear Candice's irate voice on the other end. It seemed that Gary had told Candice about the business with T. J. and the back door.

"We don't have any rules about who uses which door," Candice repeated for the second time.

"I never said we did, Candice. I only told T. J. that he would probably be better served by using the front door. I figured that way Lucinda would know he was here and could announce him to Gary and—"

"Well, you made T. J. feel very bad, and Gary will not put up with that."

"T. J. is a thoughtless oaf who ought to learn some better manners," snapped Gwen, instantly regretting her harsh words.

"Clients don't have to have good manners."

"I see," said Gwen slowly.

"I know that didn't sound quite right," said Candice. "But I think you know what I mean. You are here to serve our clients, not to monitor their manners."

"Well I'm sorry if I handled it wrong, but T. J. acts a certain way; and it makes me very uncomfortable, Candice."

"He's Gary's client, Gwen. And for that reason he deserves a little more respect."

"It would be a lot easier to respect him if he would just back off a little. Every time I have an encounter with him, it feels like a come on."

Candice laughed. "I think you take him too seriously. He's just a friendly guy. That's his style."

"Well, it doesn't feel *friendly* to me. It feels threatening."

"You need to remember that T. J. is something of a celebrity in Seattle. And that probably makes him seem intimidating to you. Besides, when you're a pro ball player, you play by a different set of rules."

"I guess I don't like his rules."

"Gwen, the fact is if you're going to fit in around here, you need to get used to guys like T. J. Now enough about that. I had another reason for calling you. I need you to go with me to a job this afternoon. The appointment's at two, but we'll need to leave earlier."

"Fine. I'll be ready." Gwen hung up and sighed a prayer. *Help me to be a light, Lord.* She finished up her work and went upstairs to take her lunch break. Lucinda was waiting by the back door with a hopeful smile. All traces of earlier tears were gone.

"Uh, you might already have plans, Gwen," began Lucinda, "but I thought I'd see if you wanted to go to the bagel shop with me. I forgot to bring my lunch this morning and—"

"Better yet, Lucinda, how about if you let me buy you a bowl of soup for lunch. Gretchen's Kettle has some really great soups to choose from."

"Well, I—uh—I guess—"

"No arguments," said Gwen. "If I'm going to be watching Sierra, I need to learn a little more about her before Saturday."

"Okay, then," said Lucinda with a grin. "Let's go."

On their way, Lucinda mentioned the incident with T. J. and the back door. "I heard the whole thing, Gwen, and I can't believe that T. J. acted like such a big baby about it. And you're right—he *should* use the front door. I just cannot believe some people."

Gwen smiled as they walked. She didn't go into what

Candice had said on the phone. But it was comforting to know that *someone* agreed with her. It was somewhat surprising though, because Lucinda had been fairly nonchalant about Gwen's first negative encounter with T. J. But maybe this was to attest to their new friendship. Anyway, it was reassuring.

They both ordered the turkey-vegetable soup with garlic bread sticks and sat down at the only vacant table. Gwen studied Lucinda for a moment. Her long hair was drooping around her face, and her baggy sweater had a small hole starting at the elbow. All the motherly instincts were rising up in Gwen, but she didn't want to come on too strong. She knew well enough from Aubrey that there was help and there was hindering. And she certainly didn't want to hinder.

"Lucinda, I really admire the way you are pulling your life together being a working mom and all. A lot of people would have taken the easy way out."

Lucinda nodded and dipped a garlic stick into her soup. "It's funny, you know, but my mom totally wrote me off when I got pregnant; and I can understand that, in a way, 'cause I know I was too young to be having kids, not to mention I was involved with a bad group of friends. But when Mom said that I was a total failure and that I would end up being nothing more than trash living on welfare—well, something just rose up inside of me and I was determined to prove her wrong."

Gwen smiled. "Well, she should be proud of you."

"She's not. She still acts like I'm a big failure. She has never even seen Sierra. And she hasn't helped me out a bit. And she can afford to. She and her husband, Carl, have more than enough money."

Gwen could hear the bitterness in Lucinda's voice. "That must really be hard, Lucinda. But do you realize that your mother is hurting herself even more than she's hurting you?"

"How's that?"

"Well, she's cutting herself off from you just when you need her most. And it's hard to fix that kind of hurt. She's missing out on one of the most precious relationships that life has to offer. There's nothing like a good mother-daughter relationship."

Lucinda nodded sadly. "Yeah, I used to wish for a good relationship with her. But now I've just about given up."

"That's too bad, although I can understand how that might happen. But you need to be careful to guard your own heart, Lucinda."

"Guard my heart?"

"Yes. If you allow yourself to become bitter against your mother it will affect you a lot. It could even impair the relationship with your own daughter."

"How?" Lucinda set her spoon down and listened intently.

"Well, you know how you said you've been really tired lately? And, of course, it's to be expected under your circumstances. But did you know that it takes a lot of emotional energy to be angry at someone? It can really drain you."

Lucinda nodded. "Yeah, I suppose that's true. So, how did you get to be so smart about stuff like this, Gwen?"

Gwen smiled. "Actually, I've learned a lot of things the hard way. And I'm still working on this one myself. You see, when my husband was killed in a car wreck by a drunk driver, I got really angry—not so much at the drunk driver, but more so at the lawyer who defended him and then got him off."

"That must've made you mad."

"It did. And I let it eat away at me for a while. But my daughter, Aubrey, brought me to my senses. She pointed out how my anger was permeating every part of our lives until she didn't like being around me. So I decided to try to move on.

But the fact is, I still let it get to me sometimes."

"Does that make it hard working around someone like Gary and Mr. Green? I mean, they actually make their living defending criminals like that drunk driver and people like T. J."

Gwen nodded. "Yes, but I think it might be good for me to work around them. Sort of like therapy maybe."

Lucinda shook her head. "Sounds like pretty tough therapy, if you ask me." She glanced at her watch. "Looks like we better head back. Thanks for the lunch, Gwen, and the pep talk. It's nice to have an older person to talk to. Candice always acts like she's there for me, but I know she doesn't really have time. Not that I don't appreciate how she and Gary have given me a chance with this job and everything. But I just don't expect anything more than that."

Back at the office, Candice was already getting ready to go. Gwen offered to drive, but Candice wouldn't hear of it. "I want you to ride with me, Gwen," Candice insisted as she picked up her briefcase and headed out to the parking lot. "We need to discuss something on the way." The way Candice spoke suddenly made Gwen uneasy. What had she done wrong now?

"It's about Oliver Black," said Candice as she pulled her car out into the traffic. "He called me today, and to my surprise he already knew that I wasn't going to do the job for him...."

Gwen sighed. "I'm sorry, Candice. But we met for coffee and I thought you had already told him, it just slipped out—"

"What are you doing meeting Oliver Black for coffee?" demanded Candice as she zipped across a crowded intersection against a light that was already turning red.

Gwen braced herself and took a deep breath. "Are you in a hurry, Candice?"

"I'm always in a hurry. But back to my question about Oliver Black."

"Well, he asked me to meet him for coffee. Is there something wrong with that?"

"Maybe. Are you trying to horn in on my business?"

"What?"

"Well, you knew that I didn't want to work for him. Did you think you could take a job with him on the side? Sort of squeeze in at the opportune moment?"

"No!" Gwen stared at Candice. "What kind of person do you think I am?"

"I don't know, Gwen. But you have to admit it does look suspicious."

"If you really must know, I ran into Oliver at the park—"

"At the park?"

"Yes, I went there to walk one evening after work. I wanted to clear my head. And he was walking his dog."

"That was convenient." Her tone was sharp and sarcastic.

"It wasn't planned, Candice."

"Okay, then, go on."

Gwen shook her head. This was so unreal. It felt like an inquisition. But then Gwen had nothing to hide. Perhaps the best thing was to get it out into the open so Candice could see that nothing wrong had transpired. "Well, Oliver was walking his dog, and we walked together and just chatted for a while. Nothing to do with work. Just a very general conversation. And his dog jumped in the pond and then shook himself off and got me all wet. Well, Oliver felt horrible and wanted to buy me a cup of coffee—"

"Smooth move on his part."

"Candice! Anyway since I was wet I took a rain check. And then yesterday we met for coffee. And he told me that his offer had been accepted on the Alvadore place—"

"You're kidding. I heard that Dr. Tyler had gotten it."

Gwen looked at Candice. "But I thought you knew—"

"I knew nothing. But the point is, Gwen, I don't like you fraternizing with my clients."

"I thought you said he was definitely not going to be your client."

"Well, it wasn't one-hundred-percent certain." Candice made a sharp right turn, and Gwen grabbed the dashboard to keep from falling on her.

"What did you tell him today, then?" asked Gwen wearily.

"Well, that I was unable to do the job for him."

Gwen nodded. "So, he's not your client then?"

"Yes, but that doesn't mean you can go out courting him for yourself."

"Do you honestly think I'm out there trying to drum up business on the side, Candice?"

"Well, I don't know. You might be."

Gwen groaned. "You really don't know me very well, Candice. If I wanted to go to work on my own, I would tell you and quit. And right now, I don't have that kind of confidence or even experience. I appreciate that you are giving me a chance to learn from you. But if this is a problem, or if you think you should have control over my personal life, then we should get it out into the open right now."

"No, Gwen. I don't want to run your personal life. I just need to know that you are not trying to become Oliver's decorator."

Gwen laughed. "I'm not even positive that I want to be his friend. He just seems interesting and nice."

"Well, you should watch yourself with him, Gwen. Gary doesn't seem to trust him. And he's a pretty private kind of guy.

Sure he may be rich, but I don't know. He seems a little unpredictable to me. Just be careful, Gwen. I'd hate to see you get hurt."

Gwen wanted to challenge that last line. It seemed that hurting her was fine if it was Candice's hand that did the hurting. But then maybe that wasn't fair, either. Gwen was just glad the conversation had ended and they were now pulling into a long driveway to a large home.

"I didn't get a chance to brief you. This is the Lewis home. I'm meeting with Mrs. Lewis. And I want you to do some measuring for me while I go over some things with her."

A maid met them at the door and showed them into a very somber room. "Mrs. Lewis will be with you in just a minute," said the maid. "Please have a seat."

Gwen studied the room as they sat on a black leather sofa. The walls were painted a deep burgundy and the carpet was charcoal tweed. "This room looks like it could use some work," said Gwen quietly.

Candice scowled darkly. "I already did this room, Gwen," she seethed.

Gwen swallowed, groping for words. "Well, maybe it just needs a little more light or something." She patted the sofa. "This is comfortable."

Thankfully, Mrs. Lewis joined them, and Gwen was ushered off to the master bedroom by the maid with instructions from Candice to measure everything in the suite that was measurable. Gwen worked quickly and quietly in the dreary room, grateful for the escape. She took careful notes. Everything in this room looked to be a remnant from the seventies. It could definitely use a designer's touch, but it would be a shame to drape it in darkness. She finally finished with the master bath and headed back downstairs.

After her comment about the other room, she was dreading the ride back to the office with Candice. Somehow it just seemed that no matter what she said or did, it was destined to come out all wrong. But in her honest opinion that room had been too dark and somber. She didn't know how anyone could ever feel happy in a room like that. If she were the decorator, she would have done it completely differently. But then again, her style and Candice's were worlds apart. Maybe she could try that rationale to explain her misguided criticism about Candice's work on their way home.

As it turned out, she didn't have to explain anything. Candice talked the entire time. She was on a high, going on about how Mrs. Lewis thought that Candice was the most gifted decorator ever to walk the planet. And how her husband was going to have her do his whole office building, and how she had recommended her to all sorts of friends.

Gwen listened carefully, politely responding and commenting as necessary. It seemed Mrs. Lewis's praise was just the medicine to smooth over Gwen's earlier stumble. Hopefully Gwen could learn a valuable lesson from this. Hard as it was, she would try to remember to keep her thoughts to herself when it came to decor and design, or at least to tread very cautiously when she was with Candice.

TEN

Gwen managed to make it to the end of the week without too much difficulty. Candice was progressively giving her more responsibilities, and Gwen did her best, trusting that her work was acceptable. And at least she had heard no recent complaints.

On Friday morning, Oliver called Gwen at work and invited her to dinner and a play on Saturday night; a friend had given him tickets to a musical that would only be playing in Seattle for two nights.

"That sounds like fun," Gwen said somewhat unconvincingly. A big part of her wasn't too sure. What if she wasn't ready for this new step? The sudden idea of actually dating seemed almost terrifying. And she still wasn't completely certain about Oliver. Although she knew she liked him, Candice had planted more little seeds of doubt about him recently.

"I know it's rather sudden," said Oliver apologetically. "I'll understand if—"

"No, Oliver, it's fine. I mean, I think I'd really like to go. It's just that *this* is all so new to me...."

"You mean going out—like on a date?"

"Actually, yes. It may seem silly, but I don't quite know how to do it."

He laughed. "If it makes you feel any better, I'm not very good at it, either. Maybe we shouldn't think of this as a date per se, but more like two friends just doing something together."

Gwen smiled. "I like that."

"Good. Then I'll pick you up around six."

Gwen met Aubrey at the deli for lunch at noon. She had so much to tell Aubrey about her week and finally about her upcoming night out with Oliver.

"Your life seems to be getting pretty busy," Aubrey said with a slight frown.

"Isn't that what you wanted for me?"

"I guess so."

Gwen smiled and patted Aubrey's hand. "Don't worry, honey, there will always be more than enough room for you. Now tell me how school is coming. Have you started up practice yet?"

"Just weights and fitness mostly. But we'll begin pretty soon."

"You don't seem very excited about it. You haven't changed your mind about playing, have you?"

Aubrey laughed. "Are you kidding? No, it's everything I've dreamed of. I think maybe I've just been a little homesick or something."

"Why don't you come home for the weekend," suggested Gwen.

"But you're watching Lucinda's little girl tomorrow and then there's your big date."

"You might like to meet Lucinda and her little girl." Gwen looked at Aubrey out of the corner of her eye. "And you might want to meet Oliver."

Aubrey nodded. "Actually, that's not be a bad idea, Mom. Okay. I'm coming home. Can I hitch a ride with you tonight?"

"You bet. Maybe we can pick up some Chinese food and a movie and just hang out."

"Sounds perfect," sighed Aubrey. "I can't wait."

Gwen ran errands for Candice all afternoon. The rain and

wind made it challenging, but finally she finished the last task and headed over to the campus to pick up Aubrey.

"Ugh, what an awful day," Gwen said as she hurried to open the trunk for Aubrey before they got entirely soaked. "Is that your laundry or are you moving back home for good?"

Aubrey laughed. "Laundry. I thought as long as I was home…"

"No problem. Any excuse to see you is a good excuse as far as I'm concerned."

They ordered their dinner and then dashed to the video store across the street to pick out a couple of movies.

"This is just like old times, Mom," Aubrey said as she scanned the classic movie section. "Sometimes I almost wish I could go back to those days."

"Really?"

"Yeah, sometimes."

Gwen made small talk as they drove home through the deluge of rain. She felt a little worried about Aubrey. She had never seen this melancholy side of her daughter. Maybe it was just normal freshman blues. She had heard of such a thing. But then Aubrey always had so much going on with friends and sports, and she was always so independent.

"How about if we eat in the kitchen," Gwen suggested as she turned on the lights. "I like it in here, but sometimes it's sort of lonely all by myself."

"Sure, that would be nice." Aubrey ran her hand along the counter as if she were trying to absorb a little of it. "I miss this place, Mom."

"You could come back home to live," offered Gwen.

"No, I don't think that would be very smart. Such a long commute—" And suddenly Aubrey began to sob.

"What is it, honey?" Gwen said as she dumped the cartons

of food on the counter. She put her arms around Aubrey, and although Aubrey was almost six inches taller, she sobbed like she used to when she was a little girl. Before long, Gwen was crying, too. She didn't even know why. Finally Aubrey pulled away and grabbed a paper towel and blew her nose. Then she sat down on a stool and put her elbows on the breakfast bar.

"Sorry, Mom. I guess I just needed a good cry."

Gwen found a box of tissue and set it on the counter. "It's okay, honey. Is anything wrong? Or was this just a good, soul-cleansing sort of cry?"

"All of a sudden this week, I started missing you and being at home, and then I started missing Daddy, and—" Aubrey looked like she was about to cry again.

Gwen nodded. "I know exactly what you mean, honey. I still miss him, too. And you know it was this time of year that we lost him." She swallowed. "It only makes sense that we would feel it more right now."

"Yeah. I guess when I heard you were going out with that Oliver guy, it made me feel like life was changing too fast, like I could be losing everything."

"Oh, Aubrey, you won't be losing anything. Oliver and I are only friends. I barely know him. Who knows, I may never even go out with him again after tomorrow."

"But he could be a really great guy, Mom. You need to give him a chance."

Gwen laughed. "Now you're singing a different song."

"I know. I guess my feelings are sort of confused. Sometimes I feel all guilty for leaving you here alone, and I want you to meet someone nice and have a life. Then I feel all protective and territorial, and I don't want anything to change. It's crazy."

"I think I understand. I've been going back and forth, too. The whole idea of actually going on a date with a man scares me to death."

"You'll do fine, Mom. You don't need to worry."

Gwen sighed. "Aren't we a pair?"

Aubrey looked at their dinner splayed all over the counter in little white cartons. "It looks like we might have to do some nuking here." She glanced at her mother. "Why don't you go get out of your fancy working clothes and get comfy while I get our dinner warmed up."

They ate and watched movies and visited late into the evening. Part of Gwen wished it could always be like this, but she knew they both needed to continue growing and finding their own way in the world. Still, it was comforting to know that they could always come back to this place. At least she hoped they could.

Before Gwen went to bed she thought about Lucinda and how she and her daughter had so little. She whispered a little prayer for Lucinda and Sierra. She hoped that somehow God could use her to help them.

Gwen got up early in the morning. Not wanting to disturb Aubrey, she quietly straightened things up from last night and double-checked to make sure her home was relatively baby safe. It had been a long time since she had thought about such things, but it all came back to her.

"What are you doing, Mom?" Aubrey asked sleepily when she discovered Gwen putting some cleaning supplies that she'd removed from under the sink into the laundry room.

Gwen laughed. "I'm probably being a little paranoid, but I wanted to make sure there was nothing down at child-level that might be dangerous to Sierra."

Aubrey smiled. "You are such a thoughtful lady." She came over and gave her mother a little hug. "You will make a really good grandma."

Gwen looked at Aubrey in surprise. "You're not planning anything, are you?"

"Not for a long, long time, Mom. Don't worry."

They were just finishing breakfast when Lucinda arrived with Sierra. Gwen invited them in and introduced Aubrey, who was still in her pajamas. Sierra clung to Lucinda and wouldn't show her face.

"What beautiful dark curls," Gwen said as she patted Sierra's head. "Lucinda, I made enough breakfast to feed an army. Would you two like to join us?"

Lucinda looked at the table. "Actually, that looks pretty good."

Gwen took their coats, and they all sat down at the eating nook that was built right into a bay window.

"Your house is very nice," Lucinda said as she took a cinnamon roll. Sierra was sitting on Lucinda's lap now and looking around with a little bit of curiosity.

"Thanks," said Gwen. "I've enjoyed fixing it up."

"It feels really cheerful and happy. I like all the windows and the light." She chuckled. "It sure is a lot different than Candice's house. She really seems to go in for all that dark stuff. Don't tell her, but I like this better. It makes me feel good inside."

Gwen smiled. "Well, that's my goal. I think we should live in surroundings that make us feel good. They don't have to be expensive or elegant, but they should be comforting."

Aubrey leaned over and looked into Sierra's dark eyes. "How old are you, Sierra?" she asked sweetly. Sierra looked at her mom, and Lucinda helped her to hold up two sticky fingers.

"Well, she's almost two," said Lucinda. "Her birthday's in November."

Before long, Sierra climbed off Lucinda's lap and began to explore. "She seems to be feeling more comfortable," said Lucinda. "But I'll stay a little longer."

"You can stay as long as you like," said Gwen. "What do you plan to do this morning anyway?"

Lucinda shrugged. "I don't really have anything to do. I thought I could go get some groceries. You know how hard it is to shop with a two-year-old. And then I don't know. It's been so long since I've had much of a life. And I can't afford to do much."

"Well, I was thinking about going to the health club this morning," said Aubrey. "I don't know if you'd be interested, but I still have some free passes. You could come along if you like. They have a pool, hot tub, sauna, and even tanning beds."

Lucinda's face lit up. "That sounds great! But I didn't bring anything to wear to work out in—"

"You look to be about the same size as Mom," said Aubrey. "I'll bet she could loan you some things."

Gwen quickly found several pieces of clothing that would work, and in no time Aubrey and Lucinda were on their way. Fortunately Sierra hardly seemed to notice. But then Gwen remembered that Sierra was used to being in day care every day.

"Okay," said Gwen. "What would we like to do?" But Sierra had already taken off for further explorations. Gwen stayed close behind, unwilling to let the little girl out of her sight for a moment. She knew that toddlers demanded close watching, and she wasn't certain her whole house was child safe yet. It seemed that everything and anything interested Sierra, a good thing because Gwen realized she had no toys. But she would fix that before Sierra's next visit.

They finally ended up on the sofa in the living room that looked out into the backyard. Today the sky was clear. The maple tree shone gold and orange in the sunlight, and bright-colored leaves were littered across the yard like jewels.

"This looks like a perfect leaf-raking day," exclaimed Gwen. Soon they had on their coats and went out back. First, Gwen showed Sierra her little fish pond. Sierra wanted to reach in and touch the bright orange fish.

"No, Sierra," said Gwen gently. "The fishies don't like to be touched. But you can give them some food." She gave the little girl a small handful of fish food and watched as Sierra squatted by the pond and carefully dropped food pellets into the water. Sierra giggled with delight as the fish popped up to the surface and gobbled up the food with mouths opened wide.

"Fish! Fish!" cried Sierra with glee. The two of them watched the fish until the last of the food disappeared and the fish went back to play among the lily pads.

"Okay, now let's go rake some leaves," Gwen said taking Sierra's little hand and walking her over to the maple tree. Gwen began to rake up a small pile.

"Leaves," proclaimed Sierra with a big grin as she stood in the center of the pile. She gathered a little handful of colorful leaves and threw them in the air. Gwen soon abandoned her idea of making a leaf pile. It was far more fun to watch Sierra playing with them. Gwen had almost forgotten the delight that children found in the simplest of pleasures. And yet it only seemed like yesterday that she and Aubrey had done this exact same thing. Gwen picked up a big orange-and-gold leaf and held it up to the sun. It was nature's form of a stained-glass window. She showed it to Sierra. "Isn't that pretty?"

"Pretty," repeated Sierra. "Pretty leaf." Gwen handed Sierra the leaf, and she held it as if it were valuable treasure. *And so it is*, thought Gwen.

Finally it looked as though Sierra was getting tired, and Gwen wondered if it was the little girl's nap time. They went inside and Gwen fixed Sierra a lunch of applesauce, cheese sticks, and toast with the edges cut off. It used to be Aubrey's favorite snack when she was two. Lucinda hadn't mentioned what Sierra liked to eat, but this seemed to work.

Then Gwen located an old Winnie the Pooh picture book among a box of things that she had saved from Aubrey's early years. She sat down on the couch and began to read the old familiar story to Sierra. Before she was halfway finished, Sierra had fallen asleep with the maple leaf still in her hand. Gwen leaned back and studied the sweet little face leaning against her arm. Long, dark lashes rested on round brown cheeks. It was obvious to Gwen that Sierra's daddy was likely of a different ethnic group than Lucinda. Gwen wondered if this was part of the problem with Lucinda's mother. It was too bad if that were the case because Sierra was a sweet child. And while Gwen didn't feel quite ready to be a grandmother just yet, she would be proud to be an honorary aunt if Lucinda liked.

After a while she eased the sleeping child into a more comfortable position and covered her with a soft throw, carefully arranging pillows to protect Sierra from accidentally rolling off the sofa. Then Gwen leaned back into the couch and sighed. How she longed to recapture that childlike pleasure that she had witnessed in Sierra today. And it was amazing to think that this little girl, who had only just met Gwen today, could rest so peacefully in the home of a stranger. Gwen longed to trust God with such a simple childlike faith. She prayed that God would show her how. And she also prayed that God would watch over little Sierra and her mother and take care of them along their precarious path. Then Gwen closed her eyes and relaxed.

After a while she heard a car pull into the driveway, and Gwen met Aubrey and Lucinda at the door. "Sierra's asleep on the sofa," she whispered.

Lucinda looked refreshed. "Thanks so much, Gwen. I had such a good time. I didn't realize how badly I needed that." She turned to Aubrey. "Thank you, too."

"Sierra is an absolute delight," said Gwen quietly. "Thank you for sharing her with me, Lucinda. I'd love to do this on a regular basis."

"That would be nice," Lucinda said as she gently bundled the still-sleeping Sierra into her car seat. "I don't want to take advantage, but it would be nice. Almost like having family around."

Gwen smiled. "It would be a pleasure, Lucinda. Consider us family." Gwen and Aubrey stood on the porch waving as Lucinda drove away in her small, beat-up Toyota.

"Thanks, Aubrey," said Gwen, turning to her daughter. "That was very nice of you to take Lucinda to the club with you. She really needs some TLC."

"No problem, Mom. I also told her about the singles group in our church. You know, they even have free child care."

"Did she seem interested?"

"Yeah, she's going to ask you more about it on Monday. She seems really lonely, Mom. I guess she doesn't have any family around."

"Maybe we can help out in that area, too."

"So, Mom," said Aubrey with a grin, "how about this big date tonight? Do you know what you're going to wear?"

Gwen frowned. "Not really, but I was hoping you'd give me some fashion tips."

Aubrey laughed. "Well, let's go check out your closet."

After a disappointing search, Aubrey threw up her hands. "Mom, you really need to get some fun clothes if you're going to get into dating."

"Dating—ugh!" Gwen flopped onto her bed. "I wish I had said no to Oliver."

"Why? I thought you liked him, Mom."

"I do, at least I think I do. I still don't really know him that well."

Aubrey nodded. "But if you don't go out, how will you get to know him any better?"

Just then the phone rang. It was Mary Powers. "I hope I'm not bothering you, Gwen," she said. "I just wanted to let you know what I found out about Oliver Black. Actually it's not that much, but I had promised to do some sleuthing. Do you want to hear it?"

Gwen sat up on the bed. "Sure. I'd like to hear it."

"Well, Ray and Oliver had lunch yesterday, and I gave Ray a list of questions—"

"A list? You gave him a list?"

Mary laughed. "Well, not literally. But you know…Anyway, it turns out that Oliver and his wife got divorced several years ago because she was having an affair with her orthodontist. Apparently she was having work done on her bite and—well, you know, these things happen."

"I suppose so."

"Oliver's ex married the orthodontist, and although Oliver really wanted to get sole custody of his two sons, he agreed to joint custody because he knew the boys loved their mother. It sounds as if he remains very involved with his boys. He spends a lot of time with them, and according to Ray, he pays quite a bit of child support for them. Oliver inherited his money from his family's timber business, but he's no longer involved in timber. Ray thinks he mostly does investments and whatnot, and I guess he didn't go into that very much with him."

"Well, I wasn't really interested in a financial report. I guess I was more curious about what happened with his marriage and whether he's involved with anyone now."

"Ray said that Oliver hasn't had any serious involvements since his marriage broke up."

"Well, your report is encouraging, Mary. Although I must admit it does make me feel rather sneaky."

"No, you shouldn't feel that way. Like I said, a single woman needs to be careful. But according to Ray, Oliver is quite a guy. I think if Ray were a single woman he'd be dating the man himself."

They both laughed at this. "Thanks, Mary. Your news was actually pretty well timed. I'm going out with him tonight, and I had just been sitting here getting cold feet."

"Well, then, rest assured. And have a fantastic time. Let's meet for lunch next week and you can give me the lowdown."

Gwen hung up and turned to Aubrey who was waiting expectantly.

"Well?" said Aubrey.

"According to the Powers, Oliver is an okay guy."

"Then I think this date is worthy of a new outfit," proclaimed Aubrey.

"But we don't have time to go into the city—"

"Never mind the city," said Aubrey. "Let's go to Rosemary's Boutique. They usually have something worthwhile. And I'm starved."

"Well, I think that little Greek café is still next to Rosemary's. Maybe we should stop there first."

"Sounds great. Then we'll find an outfit that will knock Oliver's socks off."

ELEVEN

G wen slipped the silky dress over her head. It was a deep shade of red, not quite a burgundy, but very rich. Aubrey had insisted that it was perfect for the theater. Very dramatic with its long skirt. Gwen gave an experimental spin and watched the skirt swirl out—it would be a good dancing dress, but they were not going dancing.

"Which shoes should I wear?" Gwen called down the hall.

Aubrey came into the bedroom as Gwen held up one smooth black pump and a strappy black suede with a rather high heel.

"Maybe the pumps?" said Gwen cautiously.

Aubrey shook her head. "Nope. The suede."

Gwen slipped the heels on. "I've never even worn these. I got them a while back just because they were a good buy. And they looked promising."

Aubrey laughed. "Promising?"

Gwen pointed a dainty toe and smiled. "Yes, maybe it's the old Cinderella syndrome. A pretty pair of shoes and suddenly you become a princess."

"Well, you do look wonderful, Mom. But we need to pick out some accessories. Something elegant, but understated. Do you still have those garnet earrings? I think they would be perfect. And let's play with your hair a little."

Before long, Gwen did feel like Cinderella. And Aubrey seemed to enjoy her role as the fairy godmother. Finally Aubrey stepped back and admired her work.

"Mom, you look stunning. I don't know if we should let you go out looking like this."

Gwen laughed. "It seems as if I can remember saying the same thing to you more than once."

"No, I really mean it, Mom. You look gorgeous."

Gwen turned to the full-length mirror to see. It was a rather amazing transformation. "Oh, Aubrey, is it too much?" said Gwen with uncertainty. "I mean, we're just going to dinner and the theater."

Aubrey laughed. "Of course it's not too much. You look perfect, Mom. We aren't changing a thing. Besides, there isn't time. Didn't you say he was coming around six? It's already a quarter past."

As if on cue, the doorbell rang. And with it Gwen felt her heart begin to pound.

"I'll get it, Mom," said Aubrey. "You still need to give yourself a squirt of perfume. And get your coat. I think you should go with that black velvet jacket that you used to wear at Christmas sometimes."

When Gwen came down the hallway she could hear Aubrey and Oliver chatting pleasantly. It almost seemed as if Aubrey were the parent and Gwen were the child. And Gwen felt as awkward and inexperienced as a child as she entered the living room where they were waiting.

Oliver turned and looked at her. She noticed his eyes widen slightly with pleasure, it seemed. She smiled. "Good evening, Oliver. I see you've met Aubrey. I suppose we should be getting on our way, though."

Oliver turned to Aubrey. "It was a pleasure to meet you, Aubrey. I'll try not to keep your mom out too late."

Aubrey laughed. "Well, this is a new twist, isn't it, Mom? We haven't even decided when your curfew is."

"I'm sure you won't stay up late worrying about me. But it might be a good lesson for you."

Aubrey grinned. "You two kids have fun now."

And they were out the door. Tonight Oliver was driving a dark-colored BMW. He opened the door for Gwen and she slid onto the seat, careful to pull her skirt inside before he closed the door. She took a deep breath as he walked around to the other side. He looked very striking tonight in a dark charcoal suit. And his hair appeared to have been recently trimmed. In fact, he seemed even more handsome than she had remembered. But this thought did nothing to make her more comfortable. He climbed in and started the engine.

"You look very nice tonight, Gwen," he said as he pulled the car out onto the street.

"Thank you. Aubrey was my fashion consultant."

"She seems like a very nice young lady. I was surprised when I met her. At first impression she doesn't seem very much like you."

"I know." Gwen laughed. "Lots of people mention that. She takes after her father. He was blond and tall, too. In fact, Aubrey is even going to his old college with a basketball scholarship."

"She plays basketball?"

"Yes. Another thing she got from her father. He would be so proud of her. She's actually quite good."

"I seem to recall a local high-school girls' team that took first place in state last year."

"That was Aubrey's team."

"Very impressive."

They chatted mostly about Aubrey during the drive into the city. But it was a comfortable subject, and Gwen was always happy to talk about her daughter.

"I've made reservations at the Harbor Club. Have you ever been there?"

"No, but I've heard of it."

Oliver seemed to become a little stiff and reserved after they were seated at their table. And Gwen wasn't really sure why. Perhaps this whole business of dating was new and uncomfortable to him as well. Fortunately, the attentive waiter managed to occupy a bit of their time as he meticulously told them about the specials and carefully poured their water. Then they both examined their menus in silence.

"Do you recommend anything special here?" asked Gwen.

"Their seafood is always very good," said Oliver. Not a lot of help since more than half of the menu consisted of seafood. Finally, Gwen decided to go with the salmon special that the waiter had described.

After they placed their orders, Gwen looked around the restaurant. It was quite busy, and she wondered how difficult it had been to get reservations. "Do you come here often?" she asked, knowing it sounded like small talk but unable to think of anything more significant to say.

"I haven't been here for several months."

Gwen sighed. This didn't seem to be going well, and the way her stomach was tightening up she wondered if she would even be able to enjoy the meal. They should be having a wonderful time. What was wrong? Was it her? Was it a chemistry thing? Was Oliver sorry that he had asked her out? Finally, she inquired about his sons, and he produced his wallet complete with several photos of each of them.

"Nathan and Nicholas," Oliver said as he slipped out the plastic photo section and handed it to her. "They go by Nick and Nate. Nick is twelve and Nate is ten."

She studied the pictures of two smiling dark haired boys.

"They both look quite a bit like you, but Nick seems to resemble you the most."

"Yes, in looks. But in personality I think Nate is more like me."

"And how's that?"

Oliver studied her for a moment, as if deciding how to answer. The pause made her uncomfortable. Was her question impolite, too probing?

"Nick is into sports, he's outgoing and sociable," Oliver explained in an almost mechanical tone. "Nate, on the other hand, is more quiet and reserved, and he loves to read, which is a little odd for a ten-year-old boy."

"They both sound very nice. You must be proud of them."

A smile played across Oliver's lips, then disappeared. "Yes, I think they are fine boys," he replied. "I only wish I could spend more time with them."

Gwen nodded. "It must be hard. Even though I was able to spend lots of time with Aubrey all the while she was growing up, I still miss spending time with her while she's living at college. I think the hardest thing about having children is letting them go."

The waiter returned with their salads, making quite a production of grinding the pepper and shredding fresh Parmesan cheese. Finally he left, and they began to eat. Every move felt awkward and uncoordinated to Gwen. She decided if this was what dating was all about, then perhaps she would be better off without it.

At last, dinner was over and it was time to go to the theater. At least they wouldn't need to converse there. Gwen managed to chat about the weather and the traffic as they drove through town. It wasn't that Oliver wasn't polite. He was a perfect gentleman—opening the doors, helping her in and out. But something was definitely wrong. And Gwen couldn't wait for this evening to end.

Thankfully the musical wasn't a long one, and Oliver ran into friends at intermission who were eager to chatter away about the leading man who was a friend of their son. And finally Oliver was driving her home. She was so glad that this evening was about to end that she brightened up a bit. She tried to talk about the musical, but the truth was she hardly remembered any of it. While it had been very professionally produced with talented actors and musicians and beautiful scenery, it had still felt flat and lifeless to her. A lot like this whole evening.

When Oliver pulled into her driveway, he shut off the engine but didn't make a move to get out of the car. Instead he turned to her. "This hasn't gone very well, has it?" he said in a somber voice.

She looked at him in surprise. "No, I guess it hasn't. I'm sorry. I hope it wasn't my fault." She didn't know how she could be to blame, especially when it seemed she had been trying all evening to get the conversation going. But it was so natural for her to take responsibility when things didn't go well. Old habits were hard to break.

"No, it was probably me." Oliver sighed. "I should have been up front with you when I picked you up tonight. It might have helped to clear the air. But when I saw you, you looked so hopeful and beautiful, I thought it might be better to sweep it under the rug for the time being. Now I can see that was a mistake. And as a consequence I've probably ruined your evening, too."

"What?" asked Gwen. "What is it? Did I do something?"

Oliver ran his hands through his hair. "I'm probably overreacting. You see, I had lunch with Ray Powers yesterday."

Gwen felt her breath catch in her throat. *Mary's list.*

"I felt like I was being interviewed. And finally, I asked Ray what was going on. He just laughed and told me about Mary's friend who wanted to find out more about me. I asked him exactly who Mary's friend was…"

Gwen could feel tears of humiliation in her eyes. "I didn't ask Mary to check on you, exactly. Oh, maybe I did. I can't really remember. It's just that Candice was acting so strange about you, and I haven't dated anyone since—since David. And well, you just can't be too careful these days." Now the tears were streaming down her cheeks and she just wanted to disappear. She slipped her hand over to the door handle, then turned to face Oliver. "I'm so sorry, Oliver," she blurted. "I've ruined your evening. If I had just trusted my instincts, none of this would have happened! I'm so sorry!"

She flung open the door and burst from the car. She heard him calling after her, but she couldn't bear to see him again. He must hate her! Fortunately Aubrey hadn't locked the front door, and Gwen was able to slip directly into the house without pausing for even a moment. She closed and locked the door behind her, quickly flipping off the front porch light. She stood in the shadows silently for a long while, almost afraid to breathe. Finally she heard his engine start, and his car pulled slowly away. She drew in a jagged breath and let the tears flow freely. She was relieved to see that Aubrey had already gone to bed.

Gwen slipped off her shoes and moved soundlessly down the hallway and into her bedroom. She took off the red dress and hung it deep in the back of her closet. She never wanted to see it again. Oh, what a complete and utter fool she had made of herself tonight! How could she have been so stupid? To have Mary and Ray spying on Oliver Black. What in the world had she been thinking? *Of course* Oliver was offended. She would have been offended, too. So much for dating. This was the last time she intended to date—ever!

TWELVE

Aubrey was very consoling as the two of them drove to church the next morning.

"Don't worry about it anymore, Mom. He seemed like a nice enough guy last night, but if he's going to go nuts about something like that, he's not worth the trouble. There are lots more fish in the sea."

Gwen chuckled. "Where have I heard that line before? And you're probably right, but after last night, I don't think I'd care to meet another fish. It's just too much work, Aubrey. I know you like meeting people and going on dates, but it's not for me. I really don't care if I ever go out again."

Aubrey nodded. "Under the circumstances I can understand. But you never know, Mom. Don't give up entirely."

Gwen shook her head as she parked the car. She had given up already. And she hoped never to see Oliver Black again. She would send him a polite thank-you note, very formal and very final. There was no reason that their paths should ever need to cross again.

The sermon was about patience; about how sometimes life doesn't deal you exactly what you think you need, but how if you trust God and patiently bear the circumstances, it will usually get better. At least that's how Gwen heard it.

As the pastor wound down, she mentally applied his message to her own circumstances and, in particular, the miserable date with Oliver last night. She decided she was perfectly willing to patiently bear her singleness for the rest of her days.

There were plenty of ways she could make her life more interesting if she wanted to. People like Lucinda and Sierra needed people like her, and she would be more than happy to involve herself with them. She didn't need any complicated relationships with strange men to make her happy. She had gotten along just fine during the last two years, thank you very much. And there was no reason she couldn't continue to do so. And if she got lonely, she might just go out and buy herself a cat! Lots of single women had cats. She had heard that cats made very nice companions and with a lot less stress.

After church she and Aubrey had a quick lunch, and then Gwen dropped Aubrey off on campus. She watched sadly as her daughter gathered up her bags of clean laundry.

"Thanks for letting me come home," said Aubrey. "I feel more connected now."

Gwen smiled. "Thank *you*, Aubrey. You know you are always welcome. It's still your home too."

On Monday morning it was dark and gray outside. It looked like rain. The idea of spending a day cooped up in her basement office was not the least bit appealing to Gwen. On days like today, she wondered why she had ever decided to go to work for Candice in the first place.

Gwen placed a small white envelope in her purse. She had written Oliver a formal little thank-you note, carefully worded in an apologetic tone, but in such a way as to show him that she never expected or even cared to hear from him again. She dropped it in the mailbox and sighed. Done. A small part of her was sad over what might have been, but most of her was relieved to be out of what had promised to be a very uncomfortable relationship.

"Good morning," Lucinda said brightly when Gwen came in. "So how did the big date go on Saturday?"

Gwen blinked at Lucinda. How did she know? "Did Aubrey tell you something?"

Lucinda grinned. "Don't worry, I can keep my mouth shut."

"It was a disaster," said Gwen. "And if you don't mind, I'd rather just blot it all out of my mind."

Lucinda's eyes grew wide as she slowly shook her head. "Men!" she said in a huffy voice. "Who needs 'em anyway?"

Gwen laughed. "Yes, I was contemplating getting a cat."

"Now there's an idea."

"How is my little Sierra doing?" Gwen asked as she hung up her coat.

"Fine. She kept talking about the fishies. But I don't remember seeing an aquarium at your house."

"Oh, she means the pond in back. I showed it to her. I hope that wasn't a mistake. Now I'll need to be careful to make sure the doors are locked when she comes to visit so she won't try to slip out to see the fish. We wouldn't want her to fall into the pond. Although it's only a couple feet deep."

Lucinda laughed. "You sound just like a real grandmother."

Gwen smiled. "Thank you, I think. Although perhaps I'm not ready to be a granny just yet. How about an auntie? You know, I really want to help you with Sierra, Lucinda. We had a wonderful time. She's a sweet little girl."

"I'm so glad you like her, Gwen." Lucinda was beaming. "Sierra seemed real comfortable with you too. She really needs more people in her life."

"Well, let's keep this a regular thing."

As it turned out, Gwen spent very little time in the basement. All morning, Candice had her running around in the van gathering up things that were to go to the Powerses' home—

141

towel bars, light fixtures, wallpaper bolts, and cabinetry hardware. Finally it was noon, and Gwen drove through a drive-up window to pick up lunch, then headed back to the office.

"Good," Candice said when Gwen walked in. "Don't unload a thing. We are going to take that stuff over to the Powerses' right now. Can you get that box there, Gwen?"

Gwen grabbed up a box and headed back to the van, climbing into the driver's seat before Candice could say a thing. "Now just sit back and relax, Candice," reassured Gwen as she started the engine.

Candice leaned back and sighed. "I guess it would be nice to relax for a few minutes. We had such a hectic weekend."

Soon Gwen was pulling into the driveway. "Wow, this place is looking great," she said as she admired the recently improved landscaping. "And these pavers in the driveway look perfect with the architecture of the house, Candice. Was that your doing?"

"But, of course, my dear," Candice said with a relaxed yawn. "Thanks for driving, Gwen."

Candice walked into the house empty handed. Meanwhile, Gwen grabbed a box and followed. Several workers were there—a tile man, a painter, and an electrician. It took several trips to unload the van, and then Gwen found a black felt pen and clearly marked the contents of the boxes so no one would be confused. She placed everything in the center of a room that looked to be nearly done, then set off to find Candice.

"Hello, there," called a woman's voice from the entryway. Gwen went back to see Mary coming in with a handful of upholstery fabric swatches. "Oh, Gwen," she cried. "How delightful to see you here. Have you had a chance to see my house yet?"

Gwen shook her head. "Not much of it, really. I was just

unloading some things. Candice is around here somewhere. Were you planning to meet her?"

"Not really, but it's a happy coincidence. I wanted to look at these fabric samples inside the house. It probably seems silly. But I just wanted to see how they feel in each room, you know."

"That's not silly at all. In fact, I think it's smart to look at fabrics in the room in which they will actually be used. It's the only way to see how they'll look in the proper light. You know how colors change in different lights."

"Why that makes perfect sense, Gwen. See, you even think like a decorator."

Gwen looked nervously over her shoulder. She wasn't eager for Candice to hear that sort of compliment.

"First you must come and see my wonderful kitchen," said Mary. Gwen obediently followed Mary toward the back of the house and through what must be the dining room.

"Mary, this is lovely," Gwen said as she admired what was quickly becoming the kitchen. "These cabinets are beautiful. I know they're reproduction, but they really look as if they could have been the originals, only much more practical than a turn-of-the-century kitchen. I picked up the hardware today, and it will look perfect."

She looked at a large opening in the wall next to the pantry. "That must be where the Sub-Zero goes. Nice arrangement. Candice may not be into cooking, but she really understands kitchen design." Gwen turned and studied the large open area on the opposite side of the kitchen. "Now, I know this is part of the new addition, Mary, but you can hardly tell. Those leaded windows are wonderful. Will you use this area for casual dining or perhaps a seating area?"

"I think a little of both. This is my favorite place in the

whole house. There will be a comfy chair and big ottoman in that corner. I plan to curl up there with a cup of tea and read delicious novels on dreary afternoons. At least when I'm not at work." Mary laughed. "And maybe when this house is done, I'll want to spend less time at work and more time at home."

"That sounds like a good plan. And you even have a fireplace in here."

"Yes, it's cozy, but all the windows make it nice and light. Now, Gwen," Mary spoke confidentially, "I simply can't stand it another minute. You must tell me all about the date with Oliver."

Gwen made a face. "It didn't go very well, Mary."

Mary's brows raised. "Why in the world not? Oliver is such a dear man. What happened?"

Gwen sighed. She didn't really want to go into it all right now, but she could tell she needed to give Mary some sort of explanation. The problem was she didn't want to hurt Mary's feelings. "Well, I guess that Oliver was slightly bothered by the fact that I had been checking up on him, so to speak."

"Checking up on him?" Mary's voice was indignant. "But Ray only asked a few friendly questions."

"I know, Mary. And I appreciate Ray's willingness to help me. But perhaps I was out of line to want to know more about Oliver."

"I don't think you were out of line at all. But honestly, Gwen, did that spoil the whole evening, or was there something more?"

"I kept thinking there was something more, but in the end Oliver told me that was the problem. I guess it had really bothered him that I would have him checked out."

Mary shook her head. "Well, I think he is being overly sensitive. I expected better from someone like Oliver Black."

"Oliver Black?" Candice repeated as she suddenly entered the room. Gwen felt her jaw tighten, and she tossed a look of warning toward Mary.

"Hi, Candice," said Mary nervously. "I just popped in to see how these swatches might look in the house."

"Uh-huh, but what was that you were just saying about Oliver Black?"

Mary's eyes grew wide as she looked at Gwen for help.

"Oh, it's all right, Mary," said Gwen. She turned to Candice. "If you must know, I went out with Oliver Black this weekend. And you may be glad to hear that it was a complete disaster. I don't think we'll be going out again. In fact, I am ready to swear off dating altogether."

Candice laughed. "Well, that should teach you to listen to me, Gwen. I told you to watch out for that guy."

"It's not that—" began Gwen, but Candice interrupted.

"Well, you're lucky to be out of that one. I say good riddance to bad rubbish."

Gwen winced. "But Oliver didn't do anything wrong, Candice. I was the one who messed up."

Candice's jaw dropped. "What do you mean? What did *you* do?"

Gwen figured it might be best to just get it out into the open and be done with it. After all, it wasn't such a big deal. "Oh, Oliver was a little put out that I had Mary and Ray checking up on him. But after you had said those things about him—well, I just wasn't so sure—"

"And you went out with him anyway, even after they checked up on him?"

"Of course, why wouldn't I?"

Candice turned to Mary. "Well, you must not have done a

very thorough job of checking then. If you really wanted the goods on the guy you should have come to me. I could have set you straight."

"What goods?" asked Mary.

"What do you mean?" demanded Gwen.

"I mean," began Candice with exasperation, "if I knew you were going out with the guy, I would have told you all about his dark past."

"What dark past?" asked Mary indignantly. "Ray happens to be pretty good friends with Oliver, and he thinks he's just fine."

"How long has Ray known him?"

"Well, let's see...Ray and Oliver first met when Oliver moved into town from Seattle a couple of years ago. Ray handled some business for him."

"Well, it just so happens that before Oliver moved here, he was involved in some serious trouble."

"What kind of trouble?" asked Gwen incredulously. She couldn't imagine Oliver doing anything wrong.

"It's the kind of trouble that would bother someone like you a lot, Gwen." Candice's voice sounded very insinuating, and Gwen didn't like it all.

"What do you mean?" asked Gwen.

"I mean Oliver Black was involved in an automobile accident very much like the one that killed your husband. Only Oliver was the one at fault. But fortunately for him, no one was killed, although I do think the other party had some very serious injuries."

"I can't believe that," said Gwen.

"I'm with her," said Mary. "I've never seen Oliver drink anything stronger than double espresso."

"Why would I make this up?" Candice rolled her eyes at both of them, then continued dramatically. "And I never would have told you, except that our poor Gwen here didn't listen to my warnings in the first place. Now perhaps you will take heed, my dear."

"How do you know all this?" asked Gwen. But then why should she be surprised? It always seemed that Candice knew everything about everyone.

"Remember the attorney I tried to match you up with at my party a few weeks ago, before you came to work for me?"

"Ugh, you mean that obnoxious Willis person?"

Candice nodded. "Well, at least poor Willis hasn't been charged with drunk driving!"

Gwen felt sick. Although she had been ready to be finished with Oliver, she hadn't wanted it to end like this. She still wanted to believe he was a good guy. For some reason that had been reassuring to her.

Mary put an arm around Gwen's shoulders. "Don't worry about it anymore, Gwen. You already said that you were never going out with him again."

"I know. But he did seem like such a nice person...."

"You weren't the only one who thought so, Gwen," said Mary gently. "Oliver had Ray and me fooled as well."

"How do you know he was trying to fool—"

"Gwen, why don't you just give it up?" Candice said with a dismissing wave of her arm. "And besides, we have work to do here."

Gwen nodded, relieved to move on. The less said the better. She numbly followed Candice and Mary around the house, listening as they discussed what still needed to be done and how long it would take to complete everything.

"Really, Candice?" said Mary happily. "Do you truly think we could be in before Thanksgiving?"

"I think so, but I can't promise anything for certain, Mary.

That's the best-case scenario—only if all goes well. We should have a better idea by late next week. In the meantime, keep your fingers crossed."

Gwen drove back to the office, listening half-heartedly as Candice conducted a monologue about what still needed to happen at the Powerses' house in order for them to get in.

"Well, if there's anything I can do to help get them in," said Gwen, "I hope you'll keep me busy."

"Don't worry, I will. I'm just getting involved in the Miller building plans right now, and I'm feeling a bit overwhelmed. If you could sort of manage the Powerses it would be helpful."

They spent the last hour of the day going over all the details of the Powers file. Gwen felt excited about the possibility of supervising the final stages of this project. And she felt confident that she could do it. Candice handed her the bulky file with a slight frown.

"Okay, Gwen, I'm trusting you to get this done. Of course, if you have any problems, don't hesitate to pull me in. But if I can rely on you, it will take a big load off my mind."

Gwen smiled. "I'll do my best, Candice. And I think you'll be pleased."

"One word of warning, though, Gwen." Candice's face grew stern. "Keep in mind that I don't like being upstaged by *anyone*. You are only pulling together the final pieces of the plan that I have already put into place. Don't get any high-falluting ideas about changing anything. Stick to my plans. And when it's time to get the glory, I want all of it. Understand?"

Gwen blinked. "Of course, Candice. I wouldn't dream of trying to take credit for anything."

Candice smiled now. A smug smile. It reminded Gwen of the cat who had just dined on canary. "I didn't mean to come on too strong, Gwen. But I like to lay my cards on the table."

"That's okay, Candice. I appreciate your honesty." She stood and moved slowly to the door.

"And Gwen," Candice's voice softened a little, "I really am sorry about the problem with Oliver Black. But maybe next time you'll listen to me."

Gwen nodded.

She took the Powers file home with her that night and studied every bit of it until she almost knew it by heart. She planned to do all she could to have them in their house by Thanksgiving. Not just for Ray and Mary, but also to show Candice that she could. And perhaps to show herself, too.

THIRTEEN

For the next few days Gwen focused all her energy into getting Mary's house done. She was thankful to have something that demanded so much of her attention because it kept her from dwelling on Oliver. Strangely enough, since Candice had told her about Oliver's 'dark secret,' Gwen had felt more sympathetic toward him. Oliver had seemed so perfect. Too perfect. Now that she knew he was a real human with real faults, it somehow made him more appealing. Yet at the same time she was aghast. Drunk driving, an accident, injuries sustained…well, at least she knew.

She pushed these nagging thoughts away and plunged fully into the Powers project. So far it was coming along like clockwork. Gwen had decided the trick was to be the continual squeaky wheel. She was constantly on the phone with the various contractors, keeping them tightly scheduled and on track. She gladly played gofer for them when they had an excuse that something was not in or when they needed such-and-such to complete a task. She kept them on their toes, and they called her "the Nag," but they did so good-naturedly. When it got right down to it, they really did seem to respect her. And she repaid them with lavish praise and appreciation.

On Thursday night, Gwen took Lucinda to the singles group at church. When they dropped Sierra off in the nursery, Gwen offered to lend a hand, but the high-school girls guaranteed her that everything was under control.

"Trying to get out of going to the singles group?" Lucinda

asked suspiciously as they walked toward the fellowship hall.

"No, not really…" said Gwen, unconvincing even to herself. "It's just that I'll probably be the oldest one there, and I've never been one to get involved in things like this."

"Sure, you're willing to send me, but not yourself. Fine thing," teased Lucinda.

"Well, I'm here, aren't I?" Gwen looked at Lucinda as they entered the room together. Lucinda had taken time to put on a fresh oversized shirt, but her hair still hung limply, there was a stain on her jeans, and her tennis shoes looked old and worn. There was a fairly good-sized crowd in the room, chatting and snacking on refreshments. And Gwen was not the oldest one there. In fact one old guy looked to be close to eighty. Gwen recognized a number of faces and introduced Lucinda to several acquaintances as they made their way to the refreshments. Gwen noticed Rich Cardello in the kitchen helping to make coffee.

"That's the group leader," she whispered to Lucinda. "His name is Rich."

Lucinda nodded her head appreciatively. "He's cute. Is he single?"

Gwen laughed. "As a matter of fact, yes. He also leads the youth group. When he first came here a few years ago, Aubrey had a huge crush on him."

"Does she still?" asked Lucinda.

"No. She thinks he's nice, but she has moved on. I think Rich is in his late twenties. I'm surprised someone hasn't snatched him up by now."

Lucinda nodded toward the cluster of females that were around him in the kitchen. "It looks like there are plenty who are willing."

After a fellowship time, the group took seats and sang some songs. Then Rich led them in a fast-paced group discussion about relationships. This was followed by breaking into small groups and answering some questions. Lucinda wound up in Rich's group, and Gwen couldn't help but notice the interest on Lucinda's face. Well, at least she seemed to be having a good time. Finally the small groups began to break apart, but Lucinda was still engaged in conversation with Rich and another woman, so Gwen decided to pick up Sierra in the nursery.

"Auntie Gwen," Sierra said with arms stretched high. Gwen smiled down on her. Lucinda had already taught Sierra to call Gwen "Auntie."

"Hi there, Sierra," said Gwen. "Are you ready to go?" She scooped up the little girl and located her bag, then returned to get Lucinda. When she reached the fellowship hall, she saw that Lucinda was still sitting with Rich and the woman, and it appeared that Rich was praying for Lucinda. Gwen waited quietly by the door with Sierra until the three were done. Then she put Sierra down.

"Mommy! Mommy!" Sierra cried happily as she trotted across the room.

Lucinda swooped her up. "Hello, sweetie! Did Auntie Gwen get you for me?" She turned and showed Sierra to Rich. "Thanks for everything, Rich. This is my daughter, Sierra."

Rich smiled down at Sierra. "Pleasure to meet you, Sierra," he said politely. Then to Lucinda, "Don't forget to read those verses I wrote down for you. And if you come next week I'll bring that book I mentioned. Best wishes, Lucinda."

"Thanks, Rich." Lucinda turned to Gwen, and Gwen was almost certain she saw stars—or were they tears?—in Lucinda's eyes.

"So, did you have a good time tonight?" Gwen asked as they walked to the car.

"Yes, surprisingly so. You won't believe what I did, Gwen."

"What?"

"I renewed my commitment to Christ. Rich prayed with me. You see, I had asked Jesus into my heart as a kid. But somewhere along the line I got so messed up that I figured I was hopeless. But Rich said that's impossible, that no one is hopeless. He said that when Jesus died it was to forgive all our sins forever. Not just once." Lucinda sighed as Gwen opened the back door for her to put Sierra in the car. "I feel like a whole new person inside."

"Oh, Lucinda, that's just the best news!" exclaimed Gwen. "That's the greatest thing I've heard in a long, long time." She hugged Lucinda. "I'm so happy for you."

They talked all the way to Lucinda's apartment. Then Gwen helped Lucinda get Sierra and their things upstairs.

"Don't come inside, Gwen," warned Lucinda. "It's such a mess in here, I'd be embarrassed to have you see it."

"That's okay, Lucinda. I know it must be hard working full-time and being the mother of a small child. But I won't come in. I'll see you tomorrow at work."

"Thanks again, Gwen. Thanks for everything."

Gwen had a spring in her step as she walked lightly back to her car. She was so happy for Lucinda. She had hoped that Lucinda would be encouraged by the group tonight, but she had never dreamed—

Suddenly Gwen froze in the darkness. She heard something moving in the bushes nearby. Probably just someone's pet, she told herself as she began to walk toward the car again. But she walked faster this time, too afraid to look back. Once safely in the car, she locked her doors and glanced around. This was the most dangerous section of town. Everyone knew this was where gangs and drugs could be found. It was a shame that

Lucinda had to live here with Sierra. But then it was special low-income housing, and she supposed that Lucinda couldn't afford much more. Still it was too bad. Gwen wondered if there was any way she might be able to help them. Or perhaps Gary and Candice might consider increasing Lucinda's salary so she could move into a safer neighborhood. Maybe Gwen would bring it up with Candice.

Gwen checked her answering machine as soon as she got home. She had checked it faithfully every night all week. For some reason, she thought perhaps Oliver might call and leave a message. Maybe in response to her note. But then, she reminded herself, her note had been designed to discourage any further communication. Why should she be surprised that he hadn't called? And furthermore, why should she care?

Lucinda was flying high the next day. Even her countenance seemed different.

"What's come over you?" Candice asked grumpily as she thumbed through the morning mail.

Lucinda winked at Gwen. "I'm just happy, that's all. I renewed an old commitment to God and now I can't stop smiling."

"Oh, good grief, is this your doing, Gwen?" asked Candice. "Are you bringing your religion into work now?"

Gwen stared at Candice with surprise, unable to think of any response.

But Lucinda simply laughed and said, "What now, Candice? Are you banning God from the workplace?"

Candice made a grunting noise, scooped up her mail, and marched up the stairs. Gwen turned and looked at Lucinda and shook her head. "You are totally amazing, Lucinda. You seem like a whole new person."

Lucinda grinned. "I *feel* like a whole new person."

"Are we still on for tomorrow?" asked Gwen. "I'm looking forward to having Sierra."

"You bet." Lucinda looked down at her desk for a moment. "Uh, Gwen, I wanted to ask you a favor, but please feel free to say no. I'll understand. You've already been so helpful and everything and I don't want to expect too much."

"What is it, Lucinda?"

"Well, I've noticed how you always look so stylish. And so does Aubrey. And well, last night I saw how nice the other single women looked, and, well, I've sort of let myself go—especially after Sierra was born, probably because I felt like such a loser. Anyway, do you think you could help me to clean up my act?"

Gwen smiled. "It would be great fun, Lucinda. I'd love to. Should I call Aubrey and see if she'd like to join us? She's a real fashion whiz."

"Do you think she would? Aubrey is *so* cool. When I first met her, I thought she was a model or something."

"I'm sure if she's not busy she'd love to come. This is just her cup of tea."

"I really appreciate it, Gwen. I wouldn't even know where to begin."

"It'll be fun. Right now I've got to take some things over to Mary's house, and I'm not sure exactly what's happening after that, but if I don't see you again today, let's plan for around ten tomorrow morning, okay?"

"Okay!"

Gwen saw the wallpaper hanger's van in the driveway. She knew he was hanging the paper in Mary's kitchen today. She had seen a small sample of the navy wallpaper in the Powers file and thought it seemed awfully dark. It was nothing Gwen would have chosen. Of course, this was Candice's job and Candice liked those dark colors. But when Gwen entered the kitchen area and saw how the somber paper had transformed the once bright and cheery room into a dark and depressing place, she wanted to scream. She reminded herself, once again, that she was only here to oversee and to get the job done on time. All decisions had already been made.

"Is something wrong, Gwen?" asked the paperhanger. "You look upset."

Gwen forced herself to laugh. "No, it's just that the paper is rather shocking."

"Yeah, it really changes the room."

"It's *so* dark."

He nodded. "The Candice Mallard look. You know what we call her, don't you?"

Gwen shook her head.

"I probably shouldn't say, but I thought most everyone had heard it, including Candice. We call her the Queen of Darkness."

Gwen nodded. "She certainly has a love of dark colors, doesn't she?"

"Hello, in there!" called Mary's voice from the front of the house. "I saw your car, Gwen, and I thought I'd stop and say—" Mary stopped in midsentence as soon as she stepped into the room.

"What do you think?" asked Gwen, trying to disguise her own distaste.

"Oh, my," Mary said in a trembling voice. "Oh, my. It's so dark, Gwen. I had no idea it would be so—" and then Mary burst into tears.

Gwen put her arm around Mary's shoulders. "Didn't you pick out this paper with Candice?"

Mary pulled a tissue out of her purse and wiped her eyes. She looked around the room again, then spoke in a choppy voice. "Candice showed me some samples. But I had no idea. I thought she knew. I just trusted her. Oh, this is awful, Gwen."

Gwen didn't know what to say. The paperhanger was almost half done. Candice had told her not to change a thing. Should Gwen call her now? Candice was in Seattle, but she could probably reach her on her cell phone.

"Please, Gwen," begged Mary. "You've got to help me. I can't stand it like this. My favorite room is being completely ruined." Fresh tears poured down her cheeks. "I know it shouldn't matter so much, it's just a house, after all."

"But it's *your* house, Mary," Gwen said with unexpected conviction.

"That's right," said Mary.

"That's right," echoed the paperhanger.

"Oh dear," said Gwen, looking at the paperhanger. "You probably don't want to start over? And even if you did, how could we order paper in time?"

"There's the Wallpaper Factory," offered the paperhanger. "I've hung their stuff before, and most of it is just as good as the fancy stuff. Some of it is even better."

Gwen looked at Mary questionably. "Would you want—?"

"I don't care if the wallpaper comes from K-Mart," exclaimed Mary. "I just can't stand this awful dark stuff."

"I could go work on the master bath," suggested the paperhanger. "That is, if you like *that* paper."

"Shall we go have a look?" asked Gwen hesitantly. She wondered what she was getting into.

"Is all the wallpaper here?" asked Mary.

Gwen nodded. "Do you want to see it?"

"Every bit of it," proclaimed Mary.

"Do you want me to help?" asked the paperhanger.

"Would you?" Gwen smiled at him. She had met him before at the office and knew he was one of the best paperhangers in town. He was also quite good looking. "I'm sorry, I can't recall your name."

"Tom Crandall," he said. "And I'd be glad to hold the paper up so you two can step back and have a good look."

"You are a saint, Tom," said Mary.

They went to every room that was to get wallpaper and carefully studied each one. They decided that Ray probably would like the dark paper in the study. But Mary definitely wanted something lighter for the master suite and bath. Gwen asked her a few questions, then turned to Tom. "Perhaps you could work on the study for now. I'll go on the hunt for some lighter papers."

Mary hugged Gwen. "I'm so glad you were here, Gwen. I don't know if I could have spoken so openly with Candice. She can be so persuasive and almost overwhelming at times. And I know she is very good at designing, but I'm the one who has to live here, and I like what I like."

Tom nodded. "It's your house, you ought to like it. Besides, you're the one who's paying for it, not Candice. Although you don't have to tell her I said so."

Mary laughed. "Don't worry, I won't."

"I better be on my way, Mary. Fortunately I had to pick up a light fixture in Seattle anyway. Hopefully, we won't lose any time with this change. I still want to try to have you and Ray eating turkey in here."

"It might have to be turkey sandwiches," said Mary. "And don't worry so much about Thanksgiving, Gwen. I would much rather get in later and have a house that I really like and can enjoy."

Gwen picked up the file with all the samples. It was never easy to make changes like this in midstream. She hoped she wasn't making a big mistake. "Do you think I should call Candice, Mary?"

"No, don't bother her. It's *my* house and I want different wallpaper. She's still getting paid for everything. And I will cover the cost of all that horrible dark stuff. Honestly, I'd rather pay to burn it than to look at it on my walls. I won't hold Candice responsible for any of this. I'm sure I couldn't if I wanted to; after all, her husband *is* a lawyer. No, you just hurry off on your way, dear. And if Candice has a problem, I will deal with it."

Gwen prayed a prayer of thanks as she drove home from Seattle. It was nothing short of a miracle that she had located just the right papers. She had gone with a specific idea in her mind of what would work. But she never dreamed that she would find anything so close to what she had envisioned. And in less than two hours! She drove straight back to Mary's house to find Tom just finishing up the den.

"I found them," she announced. "I went right where you suggested, Tom, and I found them. Thank God."

"I can probably get right back to work on the kitchen," said Tom. He opened a roll of paper. "This looks real nice."

"If you want to go to work on the other side of the kitchen, I could help strip the other paper off."

He looked at her skeptically. "You know how to strip paper?"

She grinned. "Sure. I even know how to hang it. But I won't offer to do that."

He laughed. "Good. A lot of people *think* they can hang

paper, but it's a whole different story when the rubber meets the road, or I guess I should say when the paper meets the paste."

Gwen laughed. She took off her suit jacket and went to work stripping the paper off the walls. Fortunately it came off very smoothly. By the time she was done, Tom had several strips up.

"Oh, that is so much better," Gwen sighed as she pushed a lock of hair off her forehead. "I wish Mary could see it. She might sleep better tonight."

Tom glanced at his watch. "You know, it is possible that I could get this room done tonight if I stayed late."

"Really?" said Gwen. "But what about your family?"

He smiled. "We single guys don't have to worry about such conventions."

Gwen felt her cheeks get warm. She didn't know why she had assumed he was married. Maybe because he seemed like such an understanding guy about the wallpaper. He'd been so helpful with her and Mary.

"Tell you what, Gwen," he began as he smoothed a long strip of paper onto the wall. "If you'll go to dinner with me afterward, I promise to finish this up tonight."

Gwen took in a deep breath. "Oh, I don't know—"

"I'm sorry," said Tom quickly. "I guess that wasn't fair."

"No, it was okay. It's just that I have given up dating."

"Well, this isn't a date. It's just two business associates having a business dinner."

"I guess I could do that. I didn't have any plans. How about if we meet somewhere?"

Tom looked at his watch again. "How about The Steak House at eight?"

"Okay, I'll be there. Good luck."

Gwen wondered if she were losing her mind as she drove

home from work. Hadn't she just told everyone, including Oliver in her note, that she had given up dating? Of course, Tom had said this wasn't a date. But then hadn't Oliver said the same thing? Maybe she should just stop by Mary's house and tell Tom that she couldn't make it. But that seemed awfully low, especially after he had been so helpful today. What would one dinner hurt? Besides, Tom was friendly and easy to talk with, and he was certainly easy to look at. In fact, in some ways he reminded her of David. Tall and blond and athletic looking. She suspected he was a few years younger than she, but what did it matter? They were only having dinner.

She called Mary that evening from home and told her the good news about finding the wallpaper and how Tom was working late to finish up the kitchen. That way everything would stay on schedule.

"Oh, you are simply wonderful!" exclaimed Mary. "I think I'll have to pop over and have a look. Thank you so much, Gwen."

"Yes, you should thank me," said Gwen sarcastically. "I am having dinner with your paperhanger tonight just to thank him for working so hard to get it done."

Mary laughed. "I can't imagine that should be too painful. He is one good-looking guy. Maybe I should have dinner with him myself! After all, he is working overtime for me."

Gwen chuckled. "Mary, Mary, Mary, what would Ray say?"

"Oh, I suppose that could be a problem. Well, it's very decent of you to be so self-sacrificing, Gwen. Especially after you swore off dating."

"It's not a date."

Mary laughed. "Have fun, Gwen."

Gwen changed into jeans and a sweater and then called Aubrey.

"Hi, Mom," said Aubrey. "You barely caught me. What's up?"

"I won't tell you everything if you're on your way out. Most of all I wanted to know if you're not busy tomorrow, are you interested in helping me give Lucinda something of a makeover?"

"A makeover? Lucinda? What a great idea! Sure, I'd love to. When?"

"In the morning. Probably around ten."

"Sounds like fun. I'll be there."

"See you then." Gwen hung up without even telling Aubrey about her dinner plans with Tom the paperhanger. Oh well, she could tell her all about it tomorrow.

The restaurant parking lot looked awfully crowded when Gwen pulled up, and she could see a line of people waiting in the foyer.

"Hey, Gwen," Tom called from the other side of the lot. "Great timing." He walked over to her. He looked different without his white overalls. He wore a brown leather jacket over a light denim shirt and jeans. When he smiled his teeth flashed white, and he reminded her again of David.

"How did the papering go?" she asked, trying to get her mind back on business.

"Great. The kitchen is finished." He looked over to the crowded restaurant. "Say, I'm starving. I don't know if I want to wait in that long line. Got any great ideas?"

"There's a little Italian restaurant a couple blocks down. Do you like Italian?"

"Sure, as long as they don't have a big line too. Want to walk?"

"That sounds good."

"Mary dropped by just as I was cleaning up," said Tom as they walked.

"What did she think?" Gwen wondered what they would

do if Mary didn't like Gwen's choices. Then they'd really be in a fix.

"She was ecstatic. I didn't think I was going to be able to get her to leave. Ray had to practically drag her out."

Gwen laughed. "That's good news! But now I wonder what Candice will do."

"You might as well not cross that bridge until you get there. There's no telling with Candice."

The restaurant was busy, but there was no waiting list. They were led past several red gingham-covered tables to a nice corner. Gwen sat down and sighed. This wasn't so bad. She looked over Tom's shoulder to the table behind them. There sat two dark-haired boys laughing and slurping up spaghetti. But something about them was familiar. Then she saw the back of the head sitting across from them. It was Oliver. And that must be Nick and Nate.

"Something wrong?" asked Tom. "You look like you saw a ghost."

Gwen shook her head. "No, I was just surprised to see some people I know eating here. No big deal."

"Oh." Tom returned his attention to the menu. "Do you have any recommendations? Actually, I'm so hungry I don't even care what I eat. As long as there is plenty of it."

Gwen kept her eyes on her menu. Unbelievable. Of all the places to eat in town, what were the odds that she would end up seated at a table right next to Oliver Black. She glanced up at the boys. They seemed like nice kids. And they seemed to be enjoying themselves with their dad. She could only hear snippets of their conversation, but she didn't really want to eavesdrop anyway. The waitress came, and they placed their orders.

"Did you want to say hello to the people you know?" Tom asked as he took a hungry bite of sourdough bread.

"Maybe later."

They chatted between bites, but to Gwen's relief Tom seemed more focused on eating than conversation. Gwen could tell that the Blacks were almost ready to leave. Perhaps Oliver would simply pass by without even noticing her. He had already paid his bill and was putting a tip on the table. The boys were acting antsy. Gwen considered excusing herself to the rest room, but it was too late. They were standing. Oliver glanced absently in their direction, then his eyes stopped on her. A look of surprise registered on his face and almost a smile, and then he looked from Gwen to Tom.

"Hello there, Gwen," he said politely as he stopped by their table.

"Hi, Oliver." She smiled stiffly. "This is Tom—" She couldn't remember his last name. "He's a business acquaintance."

Oliver nodded. "Nice to meet you, Tom. These are my sons, Nathan and Nicholas." He turned to the boys who were looking on with mild curiosity. "This is Gwen and Tom."

"Hi, guys," Gwen said, trying to sound friendly but wishing they would leave. Looking at Oliver was almost painful. She knew it was ridiculous. They barely knew each other, and she had never wanted to see him again, but somehow looking into his face was like seeing an old, dear friend for the first time after a horrible argument.

"Enjoy your dinner," Oliver said with a note of finality.

"Thank you," said Gwen. Tom had already returned his attention to his steaming entrée. "I think I've heard the name Oliver Black," he said as he dug into his lasagna. "Isn't he some rich dude?"

"Yes, I think so. I don't really know him very well."

"One of Candice's clients?"

"Sort of."

Conversation grew more relaxed now that Oliver was gone, but it seemed dull and uninteresting to Gwen. All she could think about was the look on Oliver's face. It almost seemed as if it bothered him to see her here with Tom. But that was silly. Why should he care? He had made it very plain that he had lost all respect for her when she had done her investigation into his character. She wondered what he would think now that she knew more of his mysterious past.

FOURTEEN

I think we should start our own makeover business, Mom," Aubrey said as she loaded the dinner dishes into the dishwasher. "Too bad we didn't take some before and after pictures. Didn't you just love what Michele did with Lucinda's hair with the layered cut and the weave. And it was sweet of you to foot the bill, Mom."

"It was equally sweet of you to take her to the salon while I watched Sierra. I couldn't believe how different she looked when we got all done. She really is like a new woman, both on the inside and the out." Gwen leaned against the counter and sighed. "It was like playing fairy godmothers. And she seemed to sincerely appreciate our help."

"Yeah. And it was nice of you to give her all those clothes. Some were a little snug, but if she keeps working out they'll be fitting in no time."

"I felt sort of bad giving her my castoffs."

"Those were nice clothes, Mom. If I weren't so tall I would have taken them myself. And she was really happy to get them."

"It was a good way to clean out my closet."

"I wish I could spend the night, Mom, but unlike some people, I still believe in dating. Josh is picking me up here at seven."

Gwen laughed. "Actually, I didn't even have a chance to tell you, I went out to dinner last night with a man."

"Oliver?"

Gwen shook her head. "No, he was a nice paperhanger."

"Anything serious?"

"No." Gwen wiped off the counter. "But oddly enough I did see Oliver last night."

"You're kidding! While you were out with the paperhanger?"

Gwen giggled. "The paperhanger's name is Tom. And, yes, Oliver and his two boys were having dinner at the same restaurant."

"Did you talk to him?"

"Just barely. It was all quite stiff and uncomfortable. I still can't believe we ran into each other. I hope it doesn't happen again."

"Why?"

Gwen thought about it for a moment. "I don't know. I guess because it's so uncomfortable."

"I don't know why you should even care." Aubrey closed the dishwasher and turned around and stared at Gwen curiously.

"I know, it's rather silly." Gwen looked up at the kitchen clock. "You better go get ready, Aubrey. It's almost seven."

The house seemed strangely quiet after Aubrey left. Gwen turned on some music and curled up with a novel she had been meaning to start. But before she finished the first chapter she drifted asleep.

She awoke with a start to the ringing of the phone. She groggily picked up and said hello.

"Gwen?" said a man's voice. "I hope I'm not disturbing you. Did I wake you?"

Gwen looked at her watch. It was only eight-thirty. "I guess I just drifted off," she said sleepily, then realized she didn't even know who she was talking to. "Who is this?" she demanded.

"I'm sorry. This is Oliver."

"Oh," was all she could think to say. And then, "Hello, Oliver."

"I'm sorry to bother you, Gwen. But when I saw you last night, I just felt so bad about how things went with us last weekend. And I would have called you sooner to explain, but I was working out of town all week until yesterday. And then I have the boys this weekend."

"Where are they now?"

"What? Oh, the boys? They're watching a video. We spent the day running all over the place, and I think I wore them out."

"That's good."

"What?"

"That you wore them out. That means they probably had a good time." Gwen felt like she was babbling but didn't know what else to do.

"Oh, yeah. Anyway I wanted to apologize—"

"You? I'm the one who needed to apologize. Did you get my note?"

"Yes. It was kind of disappointing, though. It sounded as if you never wanted to see me again. See, that's why I want to apologize. I handled everything all wrong last Saturday. But there's a reason. And I want to explain it to you."

"A reason for what?"

"For me reacting so strongly to your curiosity about me."

Gwen remembered what Candice had said. "Were you afraid I would find out something bad?"

"Yes. And I would rather have the chance to explain things to you myself than have you hear something second hand."

"I can understand that—"

He cut her off. "And so I was wondering if we could get together and talk face-to-face. Tomorrow, perhaps?"

"Well, I—"

"Please, give me another chance, Gwen. I know I behaved foolishly, but I think when I explain everything, you'll see why I acted like that. And then you can make up your mind about me. If you don't want to have anything to do with me after that, I will completely understand."

"Well, I have church in the morning."

"That's fine. The boys and I are going to church, too."

"Really?" said Gwen. "You go to church?"

Oliver laughed. "Actually, I'm quite involved in my church. Does that surprise you?"

"No, not really. I think it's nice."

"How about a walk in the park in the afternoon, say two o'clock? I'll have to bring Jasper and the boys along. Maybe we could grab a cup of coffee."

"That sounds good. I'll meet you at two."

Gwen met Lucinda and Sierra at church the next day. Lucinda still looked fantastic. The transformation was truly amazing. Gwen had never realized that Lucinda was such a pretty girl. She noticed Lucinda chatting with Rich Cardello after the service ended, and it seemed that Rich was taking a second look as well.

Gwen treated Lucinda and Sierra to a quick lunch at a burger joint with an inside play area. Sierra ate a few bites and then scrambled around until it looked like she was about to fall asleep in the big tub of plastic balls.

"Someone is ready for nap time," Lucinda announced as she gathered up her things and dug Sierra out of the brightly colored balls. "Thanks for everything, Gwen. I know it sounds corny, but you know how the preacher was talking about angels today at church? Well, I think you are my own special angel."

Gwen laughed. "I don't know about that, Lucinda. But I'm sure glad that God brought us all together. I'll see you tomorrow."

Gwen had just enough time to go home and change into casual clothes. At first she wanted to wear something special, but then she remembered how Jasper had showered her with pond water on their last walk. She settled on a pair of faded jeans, a bulky red sweater, and her favorite denim jacket. Not exactly a fashion statement, but comfortable. And she wouldn't be afraid to get dirty.

Oliver was already at the park when she arrived. She recognized his sage green Jeep. She parked in the space next to it and got out and looked around.

"Hello!" Oliver was waving from the park. He walked toward her with Jasper circling around his heels.

"Hi, Oliver," she called as she went to meet him, feeling strangely conspicuous as she walked. "Where are your boys?"

"They're over there," he pointed down toward the pond where the footpath went. "Nate brought his in-line skates; and Nick's breaking in a new skateboard. I just hope he doesn't break any bones while he's at it."

Gwen laughed. "I remember when Aubrey took up skateboarding a few years ago. She had a little boyfriend at the time who was a skateboard enthusiast. Her dad threw a fit at first. Then we convinced him it really was something of an athletic pursuit and required a fair amount of coordination and grace. Fortunately she grew bored with it after just a few weeks. Actually, I think she was more bored with the boyfriend."

Oliver smiled. "Well, I think this is Nick's way of reminding me that he wants to take up snowboarding this winter. And naturally Nate is right on his heels. They both know how to ski fairly well, but suddenly skiing isn't very fashionable."

"Aubrey loves snowboarding," said Gwen. "She says it's a lot more fun than skiing, and she keeps trying to convince me to give it a go. But I don't think so. I'd much rather have two long sticks under my feet and two poles to help keep me upright."

Oliver laughed. "Me, too. I guess we're getting old."

"Yes, it's probably just self-preservation." They reached a wooden table where some jackets and things were piled.

"I picked up some coffee at Starbucks. I hope it's still hot." Oliver pulled out two cups from a box and handed her one. "I think that's how you like it."

She took a sip. "Perfect. You remembered."

"Want to have a seat?" asked Oliver. They both sat down on the bench that faced the pond and the paved maze of footpaths. Gwen spotted the two boys down on the other side of the pond. Some of the large trees had already lost their leaves, but there was still plenty of beautiful autumn foliage to admire.

Gwen took in a breath of fresh air. "I really like this time of year."

"So do I." Oliver sipped his coffee and looked out over the park. "Well, I did invite you here for a specific reason, Gwen. But oddly enough as we're chatting, it seems like we're already beyond that. But I know that if we're going to continue our friendship, we need to have a foundation of honesty and trust."

Gwen nodded slowly, turning the warm coffee cup around in her hands. She was unsure how to answer.

"I guess I shouldn't just assume that you are interested in continuing our friendship...." Oliver looked at her as if expecting a response.

"I guess I wouldn't have come here if I wasn't," confessed Gwen. Her frank answer surprised her a little. But then again, it was the truth.

"I was hoping that was the case. We'd gotten off to such a

good start, and everything seemed to be going so well—until last Saturday. But I want you to understand why I acted like such a fool, and of course to apologize. You see, when I discovered that Ray Powers was sleuthing on your behalf, I saw it as a warning signal. When I realized that you were checking up on me, I was pretty irked."

"I can understand that." Gwen had been irked at herself.

"But the real reason I was so irritated was probably because I was worried that I wouldn't measure up."

Gwen looked at him in surprise. He was staring down at the cup in his hands. He swished the coffee around and around in the cup. And finally he continued. "I wanted to bring it up the first thing, before we even had dinner. But like I said, when I saw you, Gwen, you looked so hopeful and expectant, I just didn't want to spoil the evening." He laughed. "But I sure did manage to do just that."

"Before you go on, Oliver, I want to tell you something. Just to keep a fair playing field."

Oliver turned and looked at her with a puzzled expression. "Sure, go ahead."

Gwen took a deep breath. "Candice told me a little about your—uh—the automobile accident and everything."

Oliver frowned. "Was that before or after our night out?"

"After."

"Well, I was going to tell you myself. But if Candice has already—"

"Actually, Candice didn't really go into much detail, and knowing Candice, I'm not even sure she got her facts straight. I'd rather hear it from you. But before you tell me your story, I should probably warn you that I have a strong bias against drinking and driving. My husband was killed by a drunk driver."

Oliver leaned over and rested his elbows on his knees. He

173

reminded Gwen of a dejected and discouraged little boy. "I can understand that. And, believe it or not, that has always been my position, too. But I made a dreadful mistake. And I will pay for it for the rest of my life."

Gwen wondered about that. Was it even possible that the offender could ever suffer like the victim? The man who had killed David hadn't seemed to feel much remorse. He had appeared more worried about himself than anyone else.

"I know you must think people like me are the scum of the earth. I couldn't agree with you more. Fortunately for me, no one was killed."

"Why don't you tell me about it from the beginning, Oliver," said Gwen gently.

Oliver took a deep breath. "Well, I had just learned that Victoria, that's my ex, was having an affair. Nate was in first grade, Nick in third. When I confronted her with my discovery, she admitted it was true and informed me that she wanted a divorce and that she planned to take the boys with her. At the time, I was furious. I had been completely faithful to her. I had given her everything she asked for. I just couldn't understand her betrayal. Looking back, I can see that I was not as innocent as I thought. I hadn't been a very attentive husband. I went my way, and she went hers. We had been drifting apart for years. But at the time, I was furious.

"Somehow I ended up in some seedy bar in Seattle. I had never been more than a social drinker, but that night I just kept belting them down. And then I got into my car. I don't even remember driving. The next thing I knew, I was in a hospital, and later being informed of my rights. Thank God no one in the other car was seriously injured. It was two guys, and my attorney suspected that they may have been drinking as well. But the traffic records showed that the accident was clearly my fault, and I accepted all responsibility. My lawyer settled with them out of court—a generous settlement. And I can swear to you and anyone else, Gwen, that I have *never* driven under the influence again. Nor have I ever been intoxicated again."

"Thanks for telling me, Oliver." She stroked Jasper's head as he laid it across her knee. "It paints a very different picture than the one I went through when I lost David. It's obvious that you've learned from your experience."

Oliver sighed. "Like I said, not a day goes by that I don't regret that night."

"Not a day?" Gwen didn't want to sound skeptical, but she wondered if he was exaggerating.

Oliver looked at her, straight into her eyes, as if trying to see into her heart. "I have a constant reminder of my mistake, Gwen. Something I wake to every morning and take with me every step of the way."

Gwen was puzzled. "What?"

Oliver stuck his right leg out and pulled up the pant leg of his jeans. Gwen expected to see some awful scar, but instead was shocked to see what appeared to be some sort of a prosthesis.

"I had no idea, Oliver," she said quietly. "You lost your leg in the accident?"

He nodded. "Yeah. It wasn't a very good day for me all around."

"Didn't that change anything, I mean with Victoria?"

"I think it just made it easier for her. Now she had a good excuse—she was married to a drunken driver. Plus it kept me from contesting the custody of the boys. Not that I would have. I had no desire to set up a battle."

"That is so sad, Oliver." Gwen felt a huge lump in her throat, and before she knew it tears were sliding down her cheeks.

"I don't want your pity, Gwen."

"It's not pity." She pulled out a tissue and wiped her nose. "It's empathy, Oliver. I'm sorry, I can't help it."

"Oh."

"But I don't get it." Gwen looked at Oliver as if searching for more. "Why would *that* make Candice act the way she did? I mean she made it seem like you were a chain-saw murderer or something when she decided not to take on your decorating project."

Oliver chuckled. "I think she was just looking for any excuse not to take on the project."

"But why?"

"Because she didn't want to do it. I don't really blame her. It's a pretty challenging project."

"But what about the bed-and-breakfast? Why, that's a decorator's dream job!"

"Did you think I asked her to do the Alvadore Mansion?"

"Didn't you?"

"No. My bid hadn't even been accepted yet. I only asked her about another project, one not nearly so glamorous. But I figured if she wanted to do it, then I'd let her do the bed and breakfast too. But she turned me down in no uncertain terms. And that was that. I thought Candice had told you all about it."

"I had absolutely no idea."

The boys were coming toward them now. Oliver introduced them to Gwen for the second time. They all visited lightly for a while, then Gwen sensed that perhaps it was a good time to part ways. She thanked Oliver for the coffee and the conversation, then left.

So much to think about. She drove home in silence. She wanted to process all she had heard. But her thoughts were muddled and mixed with confused feelings; it was like she had just stepped off of the Egg Scrambler ride at the county fair. But one thing seemed pretty clear—Oliver was one of the good guys. And maybe now that they had cleared the air, there was hope for a good relationship.

But was she even ready for a relationship like that?

FIFTEEN

W hat in the world happened to you, Lucinda?" demanded Candice as she picked up her messages from the reception desk. Gwen tried not to look too pleased as she watched Lucinda respond. Today, Lucinda had on the plum-colored silk blouse and trousers that Gwen had given her, complete with a beaded necklace and earrings that Aubrey had contributed. Lucinda's new hairstyle looked very chic, and the gentle touches of makeup were quite flattering. All in all, Gwen thought Lucinda looked amazing.

"What do you mean, Candice?" asked Lucinda innocently. Gwen suppressed a smile as she recalled how Lucinda had done the exact same thing when Sharon had been so surprised earlier this morning. It was fun to see Lucinda enjoying this new source of attention.

"I mean, look at you, Lucinda!" Candice exclaimed in mock irritation. "You look absolutely gorgeous. I never knew you were gorgeous."

Lucinda laughed. "Well, thank you, Candice." She turned to Gwen and smiled. "Gwen and Aubrey gave me a makeover this weekend."

"Good work, Gwen," Candice said as she flipped through her messages. "Maybe I should make an appointment."

Gwen laughed, then took a deep breath. She was bracing herself, trying to think of a graceful way to casually introduce the touchy subject of the recent wallpaper changes in Mary's house, but before she could even get the words out, Candice launched into her day's itinerary.

"I'm running late, girls. I've got to be into the city by ten, then over to Fox Island this afternoon. And I won't be in tomorrow until after lunch. So hold down the fort while I'm gone. And only contact me in case of an emergency."

Gwen sighed in relief as Candice breezed out the door. She knew she would have to tell her before long but was thankful for this brief reprieve. Maybe she and Mary could break the news to Candice together. She was meeting Mary this afternoon, and perhaps they could work out some sort of plan.

Gwen spent the morning checking on several contractors and a couple of delayed deliveries. A shipment of furniture from Georgia was already ten days behind schedule, and the plumber was playing hard to get. But before noon she had most of these problems solved or at least promises that they were under control. She knew she would need to check back on them tomorrow. But that was the nature of the game. She was just putting on her coat and getting ready to leave for lunch when a large bouquet of roses were delivered.

"Are those for Candice?" Gwen asked absently as she picked up a box of switch plate covers that needed to go to Mary's house.

Lucinda read the name on the card. "No, they're for you, Gwen." She looked up at Gwen with a suspicious grin. "Who are they from?"

"I have no idea," said Gwen. "But they're beautiful. And I happen to love yellow roses." She opened the card and read:

Thank you for taking the time to talk with me yesterday, Gwen. Yellow seemed like the right color for hope

and fresh beginnings....Can I take you to dinner this week?

Sincerely,

Oliver Black

Gwen tucked the card back into the envelope, then sniffed the roses and smiled.

"Please, Gwen," pleaded Lucinda. "I'm dying of curiosity. Who sent them?"

"Well, I'll only tell you if you can promise to keep it to yourself. They're from Oliver Black."

"I thought you were finished with him."

"So did I. But now I'm thinking perhaps we've only just begun. You see, we had a really nice talk yesterday...things are a lot different than I thought with him. And I'm ready to get to know him better."

"But what about all that stuff that Candice said?"

"Candice didn't have all her facts straight."

"Oh." Lucinda looked thoughtful for a moment. "Well, to tell you the truth, I always did think Mr. Black was a pretty nice guy. And I'm sure you're a good judge of character, Gwen."

"Thanks. I hope so. Anyway, I'm not worried about Oliver anymore. Do you mind if I leave these roses out here for now? Maybe you and Sharon can enjoy them. I'm going to the warehouse after lunch, and then over to Mary's."

Gwen reread Oliver's note as she ate a quick lunch. It did feel like a new beginning. And she felt hopeful and excited, but she also felt slightly apprehensive. What if things were moving too fast? She wondered how others usually proceeded with things like this? It was all so new to her. If only she had someone to talk to. She thought of her mother, but knew she wasn't ready to involve her yet. And Aubrey was so young. Maybe she could talk to Mary about it. Mary had seemed to like Oliver, at least before Candice had defamed his character. Perhaps Gwen had a responsibility to ensure that Ray and Mary knew the whole truth about Oliver. After all, it was partly her fault that they had heard Candice's tale.

Mary's silver Mercedes was already parked in the driveway when Gwen pulled up to the Powerses' house. Running to the door to avoid the steady drizzle, she felt anxious to find out about how Mary had liked the new wallpaper. Of course, she'd already heard Tom's version, but she wouldn't rest until she actually talked to Mary.

"Gwen!" Mary exclaimed as soon as Gwen entered the house. "I'm so glad you're here. Come and see my kitchen."

"What do you think?" Gwen asked tentatively as she walked into the cheery room. She looked around and smiled. Well, at least she liked it.

"Are you kidding?" said Mary. "I absolutely love it! Didn't Tom tell you? I went totally nuts on Friday I was so thrilled."

"Well, he did mention something like that, but I just wanted to be sure. I've been a little worried about Candice. She's probably going to kill me when she finds out what I've done with her wallpaper."

Mary waved her hand. "Don't give her another thought, Gwen. I am so pleased with your choices. If Candice can't understand that, then she is not the person I thought she was."

Gwen thought about that. It was possible that Candice was not the person Mary had thought, but on the other hand it was Mary's house, not Candice's. She looked around the room with satisfaction. "Oh, Mary, I really think it looks wonderful. It's so pleasant in here. It's a delightful room."

"I don't know how you did it, Gwen. This paper looks like it still goes perfectly with everything else that Candice had picked out, and yet it feels so completely different than that awful dark stuff. How did you know what to get?"

"The truth is, Mary, I was silently praying as I walked through that huge wallpaper store. And I honestly think it was a miracle."

"I don't doubt that, Gwen." Mary lowered her voice. "Tom is working in the master suite this morning. Say, how did your date go on Friday?"

Gwen had almost forgotten about that. "Maybe I should tell you later, Mary. Do you have time for a cup of coffee after I look around here for a bit?"

"I have to show a house at three. Want to meet at, say, four-thirty?"

"Sure. Then I can give you the full story. And there's more to it than you think." Gwen smiled mysteriously. She could see that Mary was clearly interested.

"I'll be looking forward to it. Have you seen the paper in the master suite yet?" asked Mary. "He's only got part of it done, but it's fantastic. Come see."

Gwen followed Mary upstairs. "The runner for the stairs should be going in by next week," Gwen said as their footsteps echoed on the recently refinished solid oak stairs. She wondered if there would be any discomfort in seeing Tom. She didn't think so, since they had enjoyed a pleasant meal together. They had congenially parted, going off on their separate ways. She had said or done nothing to lead him on. And he had been a perfect gentleman.

"Hello, Tom," she said as they went into the master suite.

"Hey there, Gwen. What do you think of this?" He turned and nodded to the wallpaper.

"It looks terrific, Tom. You do such nice work."

He smiled. "Thank you. This stuff is really easy to hang. It's good paper."

"I just love it, Gwen," said Mary. "It's so soft and subtle looking. It reminds me of a dress I used to have. It was a natural linen with a light pattern woven into the fabric. In fact, I wore it several times when Ray was courting me. Now, every time I look at this paper I'll think of that dress."

"I'm so glad," said Gwen in relief. "I thought it was lovely. But you just never know for sure until you see it on the wall."

"And the border is so elegant," continued Mary. "I think Candice is going to like it too. It has the same old world feel as the furnishings that will go in here, and yet it's so much lighter and airier. I just really love it."

Gwen went into the bathroom. The paper she had chosen for this room was complementary to the bedroom, but with more of a striped pattern. "How about this?" Gwen asked as she unrolled a bolt and studied it in the natural light. "It looks really nice with the tile, don't you think?"

"It's perfect," said Mary. "Ray was quite taken with it, too. He thinks you are amazing, Gwen." She spoke more quietly. "In fact, he was wondering how long it would be before you branched out into your own business."

Gwen laughed. "Well, when Candice sees this, I may have to consider that."

"It's odd," said Mary with a frown. "You and Candice have such completely different styles. Please, don't say anything to Candice, but Ray and I have decided we like yours better. It is so much more cheerful. And yet it is elegant, too."

"Thanks, Mary. I appreciate that. And believe me, I won't

mention it to Candice. I'm sure you won't either. But I would appreciate your help when it's time to tell her about these changes. Maybe we can talk about all that over coffee later."

"Yes, I better get going. Thanks for everything, Gwen. I don't know what I would have done without you. And I mean that." Mary hugged her and left.

Gwen chatted with Tom for a bit about his schedule for hanging the rest of the paper. Fortunately he didn't mention anything beyond work. Gwen wondered if she should be offended at his seeming lack of interest, but the truth was she felt too relieved to care. It would have been just an unwanted stress to have to sort out another relationship.

She met briefly with the carpet layer, and then the countertop guys dropped by with the newly cut island countertop. It was the replacement for another granite slab that they had previously delivered and set, but when Gwen had discovered a large flaw running through it, she had insisted on another piece. She decided to hang around long enough to make sure that this one was okay. It took three guys to carry it in and place it on the island. She carefully checked it out as they adjusted it into the right position.

"Okay, Gwen," said Hank Gibbons, the owner of the countertop company. "Will this do?"

"Yes, it looks great." Gwen smiled. "Thank you, Hank, for all your hard work."

He grinned back at her. "Nothing but the best for you."

She ran her hand over the smooth cool surface. "Very nice. And maybe I shouldn't ask, but did you happen to bring the marble for the powder room?"

"You bet we did. Wanna see it? It's a real beauty."

"Sure, I'd love to."

The other two guys went to get it from the truck while

Gwen watched Hank begin securing the granite to the counter beneath it.

"Here she is," called one of the guys from the front of the house.

Gwen went to the powder room to see. "It's beautiful," she said as she admired the dark green slab. "Look at the pattern of those gorgeous lines running through."

"I'll set the sink in the hole to get the full effect," Hank said as he picked up the oval sink and carefully situated it in the cut opening. Gwen stepped back and admired the whole picture. Candice had found a beautiful antique dresser at an estate sale to use as the base of the vanity. It had been reworked and refinished to house the plumbing.

"That looks fantastic, Hank," said Gwen with honest enthusiasm.

Hank grinned and patted her on the back. "It's nice working with you, Gwen. You don't settle for less than the best, but you always appreciate everything, too."

Gwen smiled back at him. "Thanks. It's nice to work with guys like you, Hank, you really know your craft." She glanced at her watch. "Keep up the good work, guys. I've got to get back to the office."

She wanted to pick up her roses and check for messages before she went to meet with Mary. But when she reached the office, she could tell something was wrong. Sharon and Lucinda were huddled back in the coffee room, talking in hushed tones. It looked as if Lucinda had been crying.

"What's wrong?" asked Gwen.

"Oh, Gwen," said Lucinda. "I'm so glad you're back."

Sharon threw her hands up in the air. "I think you're just making a mountain out of a molehill, Lucinda," she said in exasperation. "And I have work to finish up."

Gwen waited until Sharon was out of earshot. "What happened, Lucinda?"

Lucinda frowned. "T. J."

"T. J.?"

"Yes. Sharon was at lunch and T. J. came in to see Gary. But, of course, Gary was gone. And T. J. started chatting with me. It was sort of nice at first. Usually he acts like I'm invisible. But today he was being really friendly."

Gwen nodded solemnly. "I think I know where this is going."

"He just wouldn't leave me alone, Gwen. He cornered me, and it was really kind of scary. I tried being tough with him, and it didn't seem to even phase him. He's such a jerk, Gwen."

"I know. I tried to tell you."

"I'm sorry that I didn't believe you."

"So why is Sharon getting all huffy about it?" asked Gwen.

Lucinda rolled her eyes. "Well, I told her all about it when she came back, and she suggested it might be my fault. She said I was probably flirting with him because of my new look." Lucinda looked down at her clothes.

"That's ridiculous, Lucinda."

"That's what I thought. Gary just came in, and I told her that I was going to tell him. Well, Sharon got all mad about it. She told me not to tell him. She said it would only make me look bad. I don't see why it should make me look bad. I didn't do anything wrong. T. J.'s the one who's acting like a jerk."

"I know, Lucinda." Gwen thought for a moment. "I agree with you that Gary should be informed. But I wonder if it would be better for you to tell Candice first, and let her talk to him. You know how protective Gary can be about his clients, and especially T. J."

Lucinda shook her head in exasperation. "Just because he's

a big-time football player. Isn't that totally insane? You know, after what happened today, I really think he probably did rape that girl. I got the creepiest feeling when I looked into his eyes, Gwen. It was like looking at the devil. I even prayed for God to help me. And come to think of it, the phone rang just about then. When I answered, it was Mrs. Sanders. She wanted Candice, and you know how she loves to chat. Well, I just talked and talked with her. She loved it. I don't think she could even tell how upset I was. And finally T. J. left. Do you think God made Mrs. Sanders call just then?"

Gwen laughed. "God does work in mysterious ways, Lucinda."

"So, you really think I should wait and tell Candice?"

"I guess so. Are you comfortable with that, Lucinda?"

"I suppose so. Although I will be keeping my pepper spray handy."

"That'd be smart. I'll be happy to join you when you talk to Candice, if you like."

"Thanks, I'd appreciate that, Gwen."

Gwen felt a little concerned about Lucinda as she drove across town to meet with Mary. Lucinda had always managed to maintain something of a tough facade. Now she seemed almost vulnerable. And guys like T. J. seemed to be attracted to vulnerability. Gwen had felt like that herself when he had caught her off guard. T. J. reminded her of a predator, preying on what he assumed was a weak and defenseless victim. Well, somehow she and Lucinda would talk some sense into Candice. This kind of thing couldn't continue in the office. In the meantime, she would pray for Lucinda, that God would protect her and give her an extra portion of strength.

Mary was waiting for her. Gwen apologized for being late and then explained briefly about the situation back at the office, careful not to mention T. J.'s name.

"Why that's just horrible," said Mary. "Gary should take care of that. I would think that he, of all people, might be concerned about the lawsuit that could result if any of his employees were endangered because of his neglect."

"That's a good point, Mary."

"Okay, now tell me all about your little date with Tom."

Gwen smiled. "Like I said, it's probably not what you expect to hear." Gwen proceeded to tell about how she had seen Oliver that night, and then the subsequent conversation with Oliver on Sunday, and finally the yellow roses today.

"Oh, Gwen, that's so romantic. You know, I had such a hard time believing all that stuff that Candice said about him. It just didn't sound like the Oliver Black that we knew. The poor man made one mistake. But, goodness, it sounds as if he has paid for it dearly, many times over. It's unkind to hold it against him forever. Of course, I think you should continue seeing him, Gwen. And if you feel like things are moving too fast, just tell him so. I've found that in my twenty-three years of marriage to Ray that honest communication is always the best route."

Gwen nodded. "I completely agree. That was something I had with David, and I wouldn't think of settling for anything less. Thanks for listening, Mary. This whole idea of starting a relationship like this feels so strange. I'm not even sure that I'm ready."

"Well, just take it one day at a time, Gwen. See what happens."

"That's good advice."

"And you *must* promise to keep me informed of any new developments," said Mary with a twinkle in her eye. "Maybe sometime Ray and I could do something with the two of you."

"That sounds like fun."

As they walked toward their cars, Gwen told Mary about the beautiful piece of marble that arrived today.

"Do you think we'll get in by Thanksgiving, Gwen?"

"It's looking real good, Mary."

"Okay, then. If you don't have any plans, maybe you and Oliver and Aubrey could join us for a real celebration."

"I would love to, Mary. But, of course, I can't speak for Oliver."

"Well, maybe Ray could invite him."

"Maybe," said Gwen. "Let's talk about this more later."

When Gwen got home, the phone was ringing. She threw down her purse and with the vase of roses still in her hand she dashed across the kitchen to frantically grab the receiver. She sighed as she recognized Oliver's calm voice on the other end.

"Did I catch you at a bad time?" he asked.

"No. I just came in the door." She took the cordless phone into the living room, set the vase on the coffee table, and collapsed on the sofa. "I want to thank you for the roses, Oliver. They're so beautiful."

"Ah-hah, so you got them."

"It might interest you to know that I happen to love yellow roses."

"I thought you might. And about the note…"

"The note was lovely, too."

"Oh, good. But after I sent it, I did get a little worried. I hope I didn't say too much. I don't want to scare you off."

"Well, I have to admit, I did feel a little concerned about—well—about things moving too fast, you know." She wished she hadn't said that. But then she wanted to be honest with him.

He chuckled. "Don't worry, Gwen. I've never been accused of moving too fast when it comes to women. But let me know if I make you uncomfortable. Maybe you'd rather not talk about a dinner date yet."

"I think dinner sounds nice."

"Okay, then how about this Friday?"

"I'd love to." Gwen kicked off her shoes and leaned back. They chatted for quite a while. She told him about all that was going on at Mary's house, including Mary's suggestion that Oliver might join them for Thanksgiving.

"I haven't made any plans for Thanksgiving yet," Oliver said with what sounded like interest.

Gwen laughed. "Okay, now the pressure is really on. I'll *have* to get that house all put together on time. Or maybe I should up the stakes and say if I don't get Mary's house done, then I'll have to make Thanksgiving dinner here."

"That sounds like a good back-up plan."

Gwen didn't want their conversation to end, but finally they reached the point where the line was too quiet.

"Thanks for calling, Oliver," she said. "It was fun talking with you. And thanks again for the roses. They look very cheery in my living room."

"All right then, I guess I'll see you on Friday, if not sooner."

Gwen hung up and sighed. She remembered how not too long ago her life had seemed so miserable and empty. And now it seemed so full and exciting. Promising even. She would definitely have to call Aubrey this week and let her know about these latest developments. She wondered what Aubrey would think of all this. Then Gwen chided herself. Good grief, it wasn't as if they were engaged. She had only agreed to go out for dinner. Who knew what would or wouldn't come of it?

SIXTEEN

Gwen did tedious paperwork in the basement all morning. By noon, she felt ready to flee her depressing dungeon. The morning rain had let up a little, and Gwen asked Sharon if she would mind letting Lucinda take her lunch break with her. Then Gwen invited Lucinda to join her for lunch at the bagel shop, her treat. As they walked, they discussed their strategy for how they would convince Candice that T. J. needed to be dealt with and how they both felt like Gary was the one to do it.

"It was weird, Gwen," Lucinda said as she spread salmon cream cheese on her bagel. "I felt scared last night when I went home with Sierra. I don't usually feel scared. But I kept remembering that ugly look in T. J.'s eyes. But then I prayed and the fear went away. Well, mostly."

"I know what you mean. I was the same way after my little encounter with him. I spent a whole weekend creeping around and looking over my shoulder. You did better than me to be able to shake it in one night."

"Well, I guess I'm sort of used to weirdos. I've had some pretty strange friends. But I don't remember anyone as downright evil as T. J. seemed yesterday. But maybe that's not fair. I guess I shouldn't judge him."

Gwen considered that. "You might have something. I suppose I've been pretty judgmental myself. Maybe we should be praying for him. The Bible does say to pray for our enemies. But at the same time I think we need to be aware and discerning.

There's a fine line to loving someone and not putting yourself in a dangerous position."

Lucinda nodded. "Like I said, I've been keeping the pepper spray handy."

Candice came in later that afternoon. Lucinda buzzed Gwen and they both went right up to Candice's office together.

"What's up?" asked Candice. "I've got a lot to do, so keep it short."

"Can we sit down for a moment?" asked Gwen. Candice nodded absently as she studied a set of blueprints spread out upon her cluttered desk.

As planned, Gwen began the conversation. She described yesterday's incident with T. J. and Lucinda and then briefly reminded Candice of her own encounters with T. J. "And," she said, "we think it's time for Gary to speak to T. J. and make it clear that this kind of behavior is—"

Candice cut her off. "Is that what this is all about?" She leaned back in her chair and sighed heavily. "You two remind me of a couple of hysterical school girls complaining about the playground bully. Don't be such wimps, just stand up to him. Like I told you before, he's a little different. Sure, he comes on strong at times, but I really don't think he means to."

"But it's more than that—" began Lucinda.

"I don't know why you are so upset, Lucinda," interrupted Candice. "You should feel flattered that someone like T. J. would pay attention to you. He could have his pick, you know. And it's probably partly your own doing. Now that you're fixing yourself all up, he might take that as a green light—"

"A green light!" exploded Lucinda, "for what?"

"Oh, I don't know. You two just need to toughen up!" snapped Candice, pounding her fist on her desk. "Just get over it. T. J. is no big deal."

"It might not be a big deal now," began Gwen with growing irritation. "But do you want to wait until it is?"

"I've heard enough," said Candice. "If you're really that freaked out, I'll mention it to Gary, but don't expect anything. I'm sure he'll think you're both just overreacting—which is exactly what I think."

Gwen shook her head and stood. "I guess there's nothing more to say." She could see two bright red splotches on Lucinda's cheeks, and her eyes glistened with unshed tears. Gwen put her arm around Lucinda's shoulders. "Come on, let's let Candice get back to her work now, Lucinda."

Gwen followed Lucinda down the stairs. Lucinda's head hung in dejection. And Gwen was certain that she was crying now. She longed to say something encouraging and hopeful, but the fact was she was too angry at Candice. She didn't think she could say anything positive. *God help me*, she prayed.

Lucinda slumped into her chair. "That sure didn't help much."

Gwen handed her a tissue. "It didn't seem to. But the important thing is that we let Candice know."

"But they probably won't say a thing to T. J."

Gwen sighed. "Probably not."

"I hate working here," said Lucinda suddenly. "I know I should be thankful to have a job. But they have always treated me like their special charity case—like I should be their grateful little poster girl, their shining example of how they help people less fortunate than they are. But they never treat me like a real person, and they barely pay me enough money to survive."

Gwen patted Lucinda's back. "It won't do any good to let it get to you, Lucinda. I know things aren't right. But maybe God has a plan here. Maybe he has allowed you to work here in order to get some necessary skills. And who knows what he might have in store for your future, but I think it must be something very good."

Lucinda looked up at her with watery eyes. "You think so?"

Gwen nodded. "I really do, Lucinda. I'm sure of it."

Lucinda smiled weakly. "I hope you're right. Not just for my sake, Gwen. But for Sierra. She deserves better."

"I know she does. And I'm certain that she is going to get it. And think about it, already she has a mom who is trying hard to follow God and change her life. Nothing could be better than that."

"That's right," said Lucinda hopefully. "Oh, Gwen, what would I do without you?"

Gwen hugged her. "Now, don't worry about this anymore. Let's just pray that somehow God will work this all out. We've tried. I think that's all we can do for now. And, of course, keep your pepper spray handy."

Lucinda laughed. "You, too."

The next morning, Gwen went straight to Mary's to check on some deliveries that were supposed to arrive in the morning. She wanted to let them in and make sure that everything was in good shape before the truckers left, and she wasn't sure exactly when they would get there. She walked around the quiet house, taking inventory of what still needed to be done— some finish plumbing and electric, a few more pieces of carpet, some touch-up paint, the downstairs fireplace mantel, and a few more bits and pieces here and there. Thanksgiving was more than two weeks away. It seemed possible.

Gwen went into the kitchen and looked around. Very nice. She still hadn't said anything to Candice about the wallpaper changes. She supposed she could have mentioned it yesterday afternoon, but after their little confrontation over T. J., she hadn't been overly eager to talk to her boss.

Before long, the plumber came and went right to work on the kitchen sinks. Shortly after that the delivery truck arrived, and Gwen was busy directing them and checking the condition of the furniture that had been delayed for so long. To her relief, everything looked to be in good shape, and just before noon she signed their papers. Just as she was telling them thank you and good-bye, Mary drove up.

"You're just in time," said Gwen. "Come and see everything that has arrived."

Mary moved through the house exclaiming in delight as she examined the various pieces of furniture. "It's like Christmas," she cried. "Oh, I can't wait to see it all put into place. Are you going to do that, Gwen?"

"Yes, according to Candice's plans, of course. It should be very simple."

"Hello in there!"

Gwen looked at Mary in surprise. "That sounds like Candice. I haven't told her about the wallpaper yet."

Mary laughed. "Don't worry. She'll be fine." Mary headed toward the front of the house. "Hello, Candice. We're back here. Come and see."

They met Candice in the dining room.

"Hi, Candice," said Gwen. "I didn't know you were coming—"

"What the—" Candice pushed past them and into the kitchen. "Did they send the wrong wallpaper?"

"No, Candice," began Mary soothingly. "Gwen and I made a few changes—"

Candice turned to Gwen. "Gwen!" she said in a seething tone. "I told you explicitly, *no changes!* What have you done?"

Gwen watched speechlessly as Candice stared at the paper with a look of absolute horror, as if she were witnessing something horribly grotesque. "It's all wrong! It will have to go. I can't believe you would do this behind my back—"

"Now, Candice," said Mary. "Gwen only did as I—"

"Where is the paper I picked out?" demanded Candice hotly.

"In the garage," said Mary. "But it doesn't matter because—"

"We'll have to get the paperhanger back out here right away—"

"Candice!" yelled Mary. "Can you hear me?"

Candice turned in surprise. "What?"

"We are keeping this paper," said Mary firmly. "I'm sorry if it bothers you, Candice, but this is my house. I have to live here and the other paper was just too dark."

"Too dark?" Candice turned and glared at Gwen. "That sounds very familiar, Gwen. Have you been over here brainwashing my client about your theories on light? I can't believe I trusted you with this, Gwen. Is this how you repay me?"

"I was trying to make your client happy," said Gwen quietly.

"What about me?" cried Candice. "You work for me."

"Candice," tried Mary again, "you should be pleased that Gwen cared enough to go the extra mile to make me happy. She has been working very hard, and if you were smart you'd see that this little gal is worth her weight in gold."

Candice scowled darkly. "So, it's come to this. Well, fine. Just go ahead and finish it off without me. Why should I care?"

"Oh, Candice," said Mary. "You've done a fantastic job with everything else—"

"Everything else!" exploded Candice. "Now nothing will go together right in here. Don't you understand that I picked it all out to go together?"

"I know," explained Gwen. "I kept all that in mind as I chose the new papers—"

"Papers?" Candice almost screamed. "You mean you've changed more than this?"

"Just the master suite," said Gwen. She felt sick. How long would Candice carry on like this? Gwen glanced at Mary and could tell that she was equally perplexed.

"Well, I've had it. This is no longer my job. You two just go at it. Have fun. But don't you dare tell anyone that Candice Mallard did this house." She turned to Gwen. "And I will speak to you later." Then Candice stomped out of the house, slamming the door behind her.

"Oh, my," Mary said as she collapsed onto a plastic-wrapped chair. "Oh, my, I had no idea, Gwen. I'm so sorry. Oh, my."

Gwen sat down on the ottoman and sighed. "I was afraid something like this might happen, but I never dreamed she would be this unreasonable."

"I've known artists to be sensitive about their work, but don't interior designers understand that they are working for the home owner? Shouldn't they want to make them happy?"

"I would think so. That's what I would want to do."

"I'm so sorry if I have messed things up for you with Candice, Gwen. What will happen now?"

"I'm not sure. But I wouldn't be surprised if she sent me packing. I've never seen her quite this mad, and believe me, I have seen Candice lose her temper a time or two."

"I feel so horrible, Gwen."

Gwen looked at Mary. "It's okay, Mary. It's not like I've been terribly happy working for her. The best thing has been helping you on your house. But look how it's turned out."

"Well, I don't care what Candice says, I'm very happy with

what you've done. If there's anything I can say or do that will change anything, please let me know."

"Thanks. At least it sounds as if Candice is going to let me finish the job." Gwen chuckled. "Want to make any more changes?"

"Hmm," said Mary. "I'll have to think about that."

Gwen went to lunch and tried not to think about what lay ahead. Right now her decorating future looked pretty dim. Candice had probably been her one big chance, and now she had blown that. Not intentionally, of course, but Candice had warned her about making changes. Why hadn't Gwen listened? She knew it was because she had wanted to please Mary. But then Mary wasn't her boss, Candice was. Oh, it was all too confusing.

Gwen reminded herself of the little pep talk she had just given to Lucinda yesterday. Didn't those same things apply to her? God could work this all out. Perhaps Candice had blown off all her steam by now. She might even be sorry. Just the same, Gwen wasn't eager to return to the office.

Candice was talking to Lucinda when Gwen walked in. She felt Candice's eyes on her, and it didn't feel like Candice was about to apologize.

"Here she comes now," said Candice dramatically, "my betrayer. I was just telling Lucinda about the way you turned on me behind my back."

Lucinda looked puzzled, but said nothing.

"Candice," pleaded Gwen. "We need to talk. Perhaps it would be better to discuss this in your office."

"Why?" asked Candice. "Are you afraid your little disciple here might be disillusioned by your underhandedness?"

"Underhandedness?" Gwen shook her head. "I have done

nothing but try to please your client, Candice. I'm sorry that you cannot see that."

"You have undermined me, Gwen, and you know it!" Candice narrowed her eyes. "I can't believe I was so gullible to take you in, thinking I could help you. I felt sorry for you, Gwen, and this is the thanks I get."

Gwen felt tears of anger burning in her eyes, but no words came. Perhaps that was a blessing. She had no idea what she might have blurted.

"Finish off the Powers job, Gwen," commanded Candice, "and then you are out of here. I'll mail you your check. In the meantime, I don't want to see or talk to you."

Gwen hadn't even removed her coat. Without a word, she turned and walked out of the office. She didn't ever want to go back. It seemed strangely light outside. Probably it was simply in contrast to the gloomy office building. At one time, she had hoped to be a light in a dark place, but it seemed that no matter what she did, it was always wrong.

And now it had come to this. It hurt even more to think that Lucinda had witnessed the last ugly scene. She wondered what Lucinda would think. Of course, she would need to remain loyal to Candice. Gwen wouldn't expect her to do otherwise. Candice, after all, did pay her wages. Gwen just hoped that Candice would be equally loyal to Lucinda.

It wasn't until Gwen pulled into her own driveway that she realized that she had driven home almost without seeing the roads before her. Her face was wet with tears. She sat in her car for a long time, trying to pray, but unable to form any words in her mind. Finally she just asked God to take care of her. She couldn't think of anything else to say.

She went inside her house and turned on all the lights. She

puttered around, doing little odd jobs that had been neglected since she had gone to work for Candice. Of course, no one would notice—no one but her. Suddenly the thought of being home again, day after day, seemed incredibly lonely. But even that loneliness seemed preferable to the stress of working for someone like Candice Mallard. She would be okay.

Gwen went to bed early that night. She had considered calling Aubrey but hated to have a conversation when she felt so down. She would tell Aubrey all about this later. It was about ten o'clock when the ringing of the phone startled her awake.

"Gwen!" sobbed a woman's voice. "This is Lucinda—I need—your help."

Gwen bolted out of bed. "What's wrong, Lucinda?"

"Can you come?"

"Of course. I'm on my way."

Gwen pulled on jeans and a sweater and was on her way within minutes. What could it be? Had something happened to Sierra? Lucinda sounded so upset. Perhaps Gwen should call the police—

The police were already there. Two cars with flashing lights were in the parking lot. Gwen parked her car and ran for Lucinda's apartment and pounded on the door.

A woman officer answered. "Who are you?"

"I'm Gwen Sullivan. Lucinda called me. What's wrong?"

"Come in." The woman opened the door wider.

Gwen entered the tiny little apartment and looked around. A lamp was shattered on the floor, a table overturned. Lucinda was seated on the couch, tears running down her face. Gwen sat down beside her and took her hands in hers. "What is going on, Lucinda?"

"T. J. was here."

"Is Sierra okay?"

Lucinda nodded. "She's in her room. She just went back to sleep."

"Did he do this?"

Lucinda nodded again, then glanced at the officer. "Can we talk alone?"

"I'll step outside for a few minutes. But we're not finished yet, Lucinda. We need your help to catch this guy."

Lucinda waited until the door was closed. "I don't know what to do, Gwen."

"What do you mean?"

"I'm afraid to give them T. J.'s name."

"Did he hurt you?"

"A few bruises. But I've never been so scared. I thought I could get him out without waking up Sierra. I didn't want her to get out of her bed and see him. I didn't know what he might do to her. But finally I had to scream. I thought my neighbors might hear and do something."

"Oh, dear." Gwen shook her head. "How did he get in?"

"I don't really know. They say the lock wasn't forced. I had carried Sierra in because she was so sleepy. I think she's getting a cold. And I had a small bag of groceries, and I wanted to get Sierra to bed." Lucinda's face suddenly looked ready to crumble. "Gwen, I'm so stupid—I think I forgot to lock the door!"

"It's okay, Lucinda," said Gwen reassuringly. "It's not your fault. T. J. has no right to just walk in whether the door is locked or not."

"I know. But it probably will look bad. He was here almost an hour, Gwen. I was trying to talk him into leaving quietly. I tried to be tough. I tried to be funny. I even prayed. But he wouldn't go. And then he started getting violent. And I was so scared. That's when I finally screamed. Not long after that, my neighbor came over and began to pound on the door. That's when the lamp broke. And T. J. took off. He knocked my neighbor down on his way out. I want to tell the police everything, but I'm afraid, Gwen."

"Why?"

"Candice and Gary will get mad at me. They'll probably think it's my fault. I could lose my job. I mean, they know everything about me, Gwen."

"That doesn't matter, Lucinda. T. J. is the one who is wrong."

"But you don't know all about my past. They could make it look like I had invited him here or something."

"Did you?"

"Of course not!"

"Then you should tell the truth. T. J. is dangerous. He needs to be stopped."

Lucinda began to sob. "I can't. They might try to take Sierra from me."

"Why would anyone do that?"

"I don't know. But I remember Candice saying how that other girl who accused T. J. had no credibility because she had such a bad reputation and how Gary was going to tear her testimony to shreds in the courtroom."

"That's disgusting," said Gwen.

"People do things like that, Gwen. I've seen Gary do it before."

"Lucinda, you have to decide what you are going to do. But I encourage you to tell the truth. The Bible says that the truth will set you free. And if you let T. J. get away with this, what will you do if it happens again? What about Sierra? Is she safe?"

Lucinda looked at Gwen with wide eyes. "I hadn't thought of it like that."

"The truth is always the best."

"Okay. Do you want to get that policewoman back in here?"

Gwen went and started to quietly pack up some of Sierra's things as Lucinda gave the police her statement. She had already decided that Lucinda and Sierra were staying with her. At least for tonight.

Finally the police seemed satisfied and thanked Lucinda for cooperating.

Gwen handed the policewoman a slip of paper with her own phone number and address printed neatly. "Lucinda and her daughter will be staying with me for the time being. If you need anything they can be reached here."

"That sounds like a good idea," said the officer.

Lucinda blinked. "Thanks, Gwen."

"I've already gotten Sierra's things," Gwen said holding up the plastic trash bag that she had filled. "Why don't you go pack. Just what you need for tonight and tomorrow. We can come back and get more later."

It was after midnight by the time they got Sierra settled in and back to sleep. Gwen made them each a cup of cocoa, and they sat in the kitchen sipping quietly with only the sound of the ticking clock in the background.

"Looks like we can take turns standing in the unemployment line," said Lucinda miserably.

"If Candice and Gary are stupid enough to let you go," said Gwen with a sigh, "well, then maybe you'd be better off someplace else anyway."

"Isn't Candice letting you go?" asked Lucinda with raised brows.

Gwen smiled. "Well, maybe she is stupid."

They both laughed.

"We're going to be okay, Lucinda," said Gwen. "God will take care of us."

SEVENTEEN

Gwen reached out and tried to answer the ringing phone before it woke up her houseguests. It seemed as if they had only just gone to bed, but the clock on her bedside table said it was almost seven.

"Gwen?" said the voice on the other line.

"Candice?" said Gwen groggily.

"Do you have any idea where Lucinda might be?"

"Yes."

"Where?"

"Who wants to know?" Gwen said as she sat up in bed and yawned.

"*I* want to know!"

"Why? It's not time for her to be at work yet."

"Don't play cat-and-mouse games with me, Gwen. You know exactly why I want to talk to her."

"I have an idea. Does it involve a certain client of Gary's?"

"You know good and well that it does. The police picked T. J. up last night. And Gary is ticked!"

"Well, he should be. And I hope he gave T. J. a piece of his mind."

"No, you idiot, he's ticked at Lucinda! And unless she wants to drop her charges against T. J., you can tell her not to bother showing up at work."

"You can't do that, Candice. Gary's a lawyer—he should know better than to fire Lucinda for T. J.'s—"

"He has plenty of reason to fire Lucinda. She was fraternizing with one of his clients, and she knows that is totally unacceptable."

"*Fraternizing*? T. J. broke into her apartment and threatened her—"

"That's *her* story. That's not what T. J. says."

"Then T. J. is a liar."

"It's her word against his."

"And you are going to believe T. J.? Even after all he has done? Think about it, Candice. Who do you really think is telling the truth?" Gwen didn't want to argue anymore. She just wanted Candice to be fair.

"Just tell Lucinda what I said," snapped Candice. And she hung up.

"Have a nice day," muttered Gwen as she hung up.

Gwen got dressed and tiptoed into the kitchen. No sense in waking Lucinda now that it looked like she didn't even have a job to go to. Well, it was probably all for the best. Candice filled the coffeepot with water and looked out the kitchen window into the backyard. Recent wind and rain had stripped most of the leaves off the big maple. And with the gray sky hanging low, the backyard looked bleak and drab. Most of the flowers were brown and dying, and the lawn was littered with soggy leaves. Typical November.

Gwen sighed and wondered how to proceed with her life. Candice had made it clear that she was no longer wanted, but just the same, she expected Gwen to finish Mary's house. And Gwen wanted to do that, for Mary's sake more than Candice's. But it would be tricky avoiding Candice in the process. Fortunately she had kept the Powers file in her car so she would not need to go into the office today. She could do any phoning from home or Mary's. Most of all she needed to bring things over from the warehouse and slowly start getting furnishings and things into place. And maybe Lucinda could help out with some of that. Gwen could just add Lucinda's hours to the Powerses' bill.

"Good morning," said Lucinda. "I overslept."

"Good morning, Lucinda. I hope you slept okay, especially after last night's ordeal."

"Actually, I did. Sierra is still asleep. I hate to wake her."

"Well, then don't." Gwen poured a cup of coffee and handed it to her. "Candice called a few minutes ago."

"Oh..." Lucinda's eyes grew wide as she sipped the coffee. "So, I'm guessing they heard the news."

Gwen nodded. "Candice has given you an ultimatum."

"Yeah?"

"Basically it's drop the charges or be fired."

"It figures." Lucinda sat down at the breakfast bar and put her head in her hands and groaned. "Just when life starts to look good. I feel like I'm just getting back on track, recommitting my life to God, starting to care about my appearance.... I had even cleaned my apartment, not that you could tell after T. J. made a mess of it." Lucinda shook her head sadly. "It just figures..."

"Lucinda, you're going to be fine. Don't ask me how, but I just know it. You and Sierra have me, and more importantly you have God. This little juncture is not going to be a dead end. In fact, I'll bet you that it's going to be a turning point."

Lucinda looked up. "A turning point?"

"Yes, you said yourself that you hated your job with Candice and Gary. So now we'll just have to find you something better."

"But who would want to hire me?"

"Lots of people, Lucinda. You're bright and young. And when you put your mind to it, you're a real hard worker. I've seen you."

"But Gwen, you don't know everything about me." Lucinda looked down at her mug and continued in a quiet voice. "You probably don't know that I have a record with the police. It wasn't really my fault, but I was with Sierra's dad when it happened. That's how I ended up with Candice and Gary. They defended Darren. I was pregnant at the time, and Gary felt sorry for me. He helped to get me off. And then he actually offered me a job. His other receptionist had walked out without giving any notice. He said since I was tough and street-smart that I would be a good one to handle that desk." She laughed sarcastically. "Sharon said that the other receptionist left because she got fed up with some of Gary's shady clients."

Gwen took a sip of coffee. "You don't have to answer if you don't want to, but I am curious. What did Sierra's daddy do that got him in trouble?"

"Well, we were really strapped for cash. Darren would never admit it, but I'm pretty certain he was doing drugs. I had been working as a desk clerk at a hotel, but I had such bad morning sickness with Sierra that finally I couldn't work." Lucinda clenched her fists. "And Darren never worked at a regular job. He was from a rich family—he didn't think he needed to work."

"Did you love him?"

"I guess I was sort of infatuated with him—at first. He used to come into the hotel dressed really nice. And he was good looking. I liked his attention. Anyway, one thing led to another. And it ended with him robbing a convenience store while I waited in the car. He said he was going in for cigarettes." Lucinda sighed. "But it's still on my record. Accomplice to first degree robbery and assault, I think that's what it is. Not very pretty."

Gwen nodded. "I see. So for that reason you might feel like your only hope for financial security would be for you to remain with Candice and Gary. But is that what you want to do?"

"Of course not."

"Well, then don't give in to their threat. Somehow we'll get by, Lucinda. There are people out there who are willing to give you a chance. In the meantime, I'll help you."

Tears were sliding down Lucinda's cheeks now. "Thanks, Gwen. I hope someday I can repay you for all you've done for me."

"Like you said, we can take turns waiting in the unemployment line."

They both laughed.

Gwen made several phone calls and then went over to Mary's house to see how the plumber had progressed. The electrician was coming at the end of the week. And it looked like the furnishings could be set into place by next week. Everything was running like clockwork. Well almost. Gwen tried not to think about the mess with Candice as she made a to-do list for the handyman who would be coming on Friday to install towel bars and such.

"Oh, Gwen," called Mary. "You're here. Did Candice finally cool down? I told Ray and he couldn't believe it. How is it going?"

"Well, as far as your house, it's going great. But Candice didn't cool down. As a matter of fact, she fired me, effective as soon as your house is finished."

"No!" Mary shook her head. "That woman is insane."

Gwen forced a laugh. "She is a little eccentric, but I don't think she's insane. But let's not talk about her anymore. It will only depress me. I think you can start moving your things in next week. I'd like to have you around to consult with when I start placing things. I know Candice has plans, but I'd like to have your involvement, too."

They talked for a while about what days and times were best for Mary and some things that Mary wanted to see done. Just as they were finishing up, they heard Ray calling.

"Oops, I almost forgot," said Mary. "Ray is dropping by with Oliver."

"Oliver?"

"Yes, I hope you don't mind. He wanted to see our place."

"Hello, ladies," said Ray. "I promised Oliver a little tour before we go to lunch. Say, maybe you two would like to join us."

"Yes," agreed Oliver. "That's a great idea." His eyes met Gwen's. It was like looking out on the ocean on a sunny day, and Gwen suddenly felt herself smiling.

"Sure," said Mary. "That is if you're free, Gwen?"

Gwen laughed. "Well, you know exactly how free I am."

Mary turned to Ray and said quietly. "You won't believe what Candice has gone and done." Then she put her hand over her mouth and turned back to Gwen. "But I won't say another word—"

"It's okay, Mary. Pretty soon the whole town will know anyway. It might as well start here. At least that way, the rumor might have a better chance of being correct."

"Well," began Mary dramatically. "After the way Gwen has helped us, literally saving the day as far as I'm concerned, Candice has gone and given her the boot."

"You're not serious," said Ray.

Mary nodded. "I'm sure she resents Gwen's abilities. Gwen is probably a better decorator than Candice—"

"Oh, I wouldn't say that—"

"You don't have to," interrupted Ray. "I've already said as much myself."

Oliver grinned. "You've got my vote, too, Gwen."

"Thanks," said Gwen. "It's nice to hear something good. It's not easy getting fired."

After Oliver's tour they all enjoyed a leisurely lunch. It was encouraging to chat and laugh with friends. The last twenty-four hours had felt like a bad dream, and as much as she had tried to be positive with Lucinda, she had been fighting self-doubt the whole time herself. Ray and Mary parted ways in the parking lot, but Oliver lingered for a moment.

"Gwen," he began. "Now that you are a free agent, so to speak, how about looking at a job for me?"

"Really?"

"Yes. It's the same job that Candice turned her nose up at. And you may not be interested. It's certainly not glamorous."

"I don't care about glamour. I'd love to see it. Do you really think I'd be up to it?"

"I do. If you have time right now, I'm on my way over there to meet with a guy."

"Sure. Things are under control at Mary's. And I'm not eager to go back to the office."

Oliver shook his head. "I can't believe Candice would let you go. But I think you'll be better off without her."

They talked comfortably as Oliver drove through town. She asked about his boys and Jasper, and then she told him the whole story of Lucinda.

"She's fortunate to have you, Gwen," he said solemnly.

"I suppose so. But I feel pretty fortunate to have her, too. I think I needed someone to need me just as bad as she needed someone."

She saw him smile. And it warmed her like sunshine. She wasn't sure where he was going, but it looked like they weren't too far from where Lucinda's apartment complex was located. Gwen hadn't been down this way much before. She had always heard it was the rough side of town.

Oliver parked in front of a large building that was standing off by itself. "I guess I should have explained a little more about this project, but we were having such a good visit.… Anyway, a friend of mine—" he glanced up and down the street—"should be meeting us here. He's been doing some volunteer work with the Front Street Mission."

"I've heard of that," said Gwen. "I saw a little article in our church newsletter about how they really reach out to the poor and that the mission is growing quickly."

Oliver nodded. "This guy has a real vision to help troubled teens—runaways in particular. Anyway, I met him at a meeting and we've become good friends; I suppose I've caught some of his vision. He wants to create a place where kids could stay separate from adults—a safe place where they could get help and put their lives back together with counselors and people who care. So I bought this building a couple months ago. As you can see, I've already had some refurbishing done—mostly to the outside, the roof, and the heating system. But I had asked Candice about giving me some help for the inside. I want it to be a place where kids feel at home and comfortable. Well, as you know, Candice turned me down cold. I wasn't all that surprised. But Ray had suggested her and I gave it a try. I think she was insulted when I showed it to her. She had thought I was going to ask her to do the Alvadore Mansion—which I might have if she had been willing to do this—"

"Hi there!" called a man walking toward them. "I parked in back. I was just looking around."

Gwen blinked in surprise.

"Gwen, meet Rich Cardello," Oliver said as he clasped his friend's hand.

"I already know him," Gwen said as she shook Rich's hand. "I had no idea you were involved in this, Rich. What a pleasant surprise."

"Good to see you, Gwen. Yes, I guess this is sort of like my secret life. We call it Jericho House." His brown eyes sparkled with enthusiasm. "It's exciting to see it finally starting to fall into place."

"Oliver has been telling me a little about it. I think it sounds great."

"You probably already know that Gwen is an interior designer," explained Oliver. "I've asked her to have a look inside."

"Well, I'm not actually a designer," said Gwen apologetically. "But I know a little about it. And I'm happy to share my thoughts."

"That's what I was hoping," said Oliver.

They walked through the entire building. During the tour, Gwen made numerous suggestions and tossed out dozens of ideas. Oliver and Rich both nodded in agreement.

"Gwen, I think you understand the look we hope to achieve," Rich said as he finally locked the door.

"Well, I guess I'm very partial to light and comforting colors—I like open spaces that are still cozy and cheerful."

"That sounds just right," said Oliver. "Are you interested in this project?"

"Are you kidding? I would love to do this. I would do this project for free. In fact, I'd probably even pay you to let me do this."

Oliver laughed. "Well, I don't think that's necessary. But we wouldn't mind getting a good deal. We also wouldn't mind if you could do a good job on it without spending a fortune."

Gwen smiled. "That's my favorite way to decorate. I've never felt it was imperative to pay a lot to have nice decor."

Oliver reached out to shake her hand. "Do we have an agreement then?"

She looked into his eyes and eagerly shook his hand. "You bet! Of course, I won't be able to start on it until I get Mary's house all put together, but that should be pretty much done by next week."

Oliver glanced over at Rich. "By the way, Gwen has a friend who might be looking for a job. Her name is Lucinda and she has fallen on some hard times, but she's a good receptionist."

Rich laughed. "It is a small world."

"Rich has already met Lucinda," explained Gwen.

"So what do you think?" asked Oliver.

"I think we should put Lucinda to work," said Rich.

"Really?" said Gwen. "Just like that?"

"Well, maybe she'd like to have something to say about it," said Rich with a grin. "But I'm willing to give her a try."

"I can't wait to tell Lucinda," Gwen said as they drove away. "This feels like a brand-new beginning."

"Maybe it is," said Oliver. "I've found that God is amazing when it comes to bringing joy out of sorrow or using evil to make something good."

"That's what I was just thinking."

EIGHTEEN

Ray and Mary Powers had a full house for Thanksgiving dinner. Gwen brought Aubrey and Lucinda and Sierra. And, of course, Oliver was there.

"I thought that getting Mary's house finished was supposed to get you off from having to cook the turkey," Oliver teased as Gwen basted the twenty-seven-pound bird.

She laughed. "I offered to do this."

"Yes," said Mary. "And you should be thankful, Oliver Black."

"That's right," agreed Mary's son, Bradley. "Mom can do some pretty wicked things to turkeys. I can guarantee that you wouldn't want to see it."

"Out of here, you!" Mary said as she shooed her tall son away. "Why don't you make yourself useful and take Aubrey on a tour of the house." She glanced at Lucinda. "I'm sure you've already seen more than enough of it to last you for a while."

Lucinda laughed. "Not at all. I loved every minute I worked here helping Gwen. It is such a beautiful house, Mary. It must be wonderful to finally be in."

"Thanks to you and Gwen," said Mary with a big smile.

"Mary, your house looks absolutely fantastic," said Shawna Stevens, a friend of Mary. "And this kitchen area is so nice. It's so cheerful and light. Did I hear that Candice Mallard was your decorator?"

"Well, Candice started it, but Gwen finished it. Now Gwen

is working on her own. She's really good." Mary winked at Gwen.

"I'll have to get your card, Gwen," said Shawna. "I've got a room that needs a special touch."

"I already have Gwen booked for the next several months," said Oliver. "She's doing a big project for me. I have a feeling she's going to be a very busy lady."

"Then I better make sure I get scheduled," said Shawna.

"We'll have to talk," said Gwen.

"You need to get some business cards printed up," whispered Oliver as soon as Shawna was out of earshot.

"I guess so. But I don't want to mislead anyone. I'll have to make it clear that I don't have any fancy degrees or impressive training."

"Some things can't be taught," he said as he sneaked another olive. "They don't give out degrees for your type of gifts and instincts, Gwen."

"I suppose not." Gwen smiled up at him. In the last two weeks she and Oliver had become closer than ever. It was hard to believe now that she had ever been worried about embarking on a relationship with him. Now she couldn't imagine life without Oliver Black.

"I know *I'm* not worried about your decorating abilities." Oliver pushed a loose strand of hair away from her eyes, allowing his hand to linger on her cheek for a moment. "I have complete confidence in you, Gwen."

Gwen felt her cheeks growing warm and glanced around to see if anyone else was watching, but the others had moved from the kitchen into the formal dining room. "I'll do my best not to let you down," she said in a voice that sounded stiff to her ears.

"And I'll do the same," said Oliver in a serious voice. His eyes looked into hers with surprising intensity.

Gwen glanced away, not knowing quite how to respond. She felt caught off guard, and her heart was racing ahead. Were they still talking about work?

He reached out and took her hand in his. "I'm not referring to a business relationship right now." He grinned and his eyes twinkled with mischief and promise.

Gwen sighed in relief. They were on the same track, after all! She squeezed his hand and smiled. "I was hoping you weren't."

"Hey, Oliver," called Ray from the den where the football game was playing on the big-screen television. "You gotta see this!"

"We'll finish this conversation later," said Oliver. Then he leaned over and let his lips gently brush the side of her face. Gwen nodded, then turned back to the oven as he left the kitchen. Her hand reached up to touch the spot on her cheek as if to seal Oliver's kiss.

"Mom, you did a great job," said Aubrey. Gwen spun around to see her daughter smiling with pride. "I always knew you were talented, but I really had no idea. Bradley showed me the whole house. It's terrific!"

"Well, I can't take all the credit," said Gwen. "Candice really did most of the designing. I just did the putting together and a little fine-tuning at the end."

"Well, it probably would look even better if you had done it from the start," said Aubrey quietly.

Just then Lucinda came into the kitchen. "I totally agree with you, Aubrey, but let's not tell Mary. She's enjoying it so much as it is."

"You two!" scolded Gwen.

"Hey, did you hear about T J.?" asked Lucinda in a confidential tone.

"No," said Gwen. "What's up?"

"He's talking about making a guilty plea before prosecution begins."

"You're kidding! I can't believe Gary would even allow that."

Lucinda nodded. "Rich Cardello has been meeting with T. J. and apparently has made quite an impression on him. He said T. J.'s finally admitting that he has a problem and needs help."

"That's amazing," said Aubrey. "Do you think he's sincere?"

"I don't know, but Rich said there's not a real strong case against him, and Gary could probably get him off, so for T.J. to consider this is something."

"How do you feel about that, Lucinda?" asked Gwen.

"I'm glad he wants to tell the truth. And I'm even more glad that he's meeting with Rich."

"It sounds as if you've been meeting with Rich, too."

Lucinda smiled. "I guess you could say that."

As the large happy group gathered around the huge table in the dining room, Gwen compared it to another dinner party she had attended not all that long ago. And yet, to her, it was another lifetime. She remembered how she had felt at Candice's dinner party that night. Life had seemed hopeless, pointless, empty. And then when Candice had reluctantly offered her that job, it was as if a small door opened. Things had not all gone well; there had been times when she had been perfectly miserable. But somehow God had used it all—the good and the bad—to bring her to a new place. A new beginning. It was as if, after the long, dark night, the sun was beginning to peek over the horizon. And shades of darkness had been transformed into shades of light.

Sullivan-Black Wedding

In the recently and beautifully refurbished historical Alvadore Mansion, Gwen Elizabeth Sullivan and Oliver Terrence Black repeated marriage vows. Pastor Rich Cardello officiated the ceremony. The bride wore a full-length gown of white satin and lace and carried yellow and white roses. The bride's daughter, Aubrey Sullivan, stood as maid of honor, and Lucinda Cardello and Mary Powers joined as attendants. They wore pale green satin gowns and carried yellow rosebuds. Flower girl Sierra Cardello carried daisies and wore a dress of yellow organdy. The groom's best man was Ray Powers and serving as ushers were the groom's two sons, Nathan and Nicholas Black. The bride and groom will enjoy a honeymoon trip to Europe and will return to reside in the Alvadore Mansion. There are rumors that the newlyweds will someday turn the mansion into a bed-and-breakfast, but Oliver Black says that for now they just want to enjoy the beautifully restored mansion that his talented wife worked so hard to finish in time for the wedding.

Dear Reader,

We all go through changes in our lives. Sometimes more often than we like. But the good news is that God never changes. He is the same yesterday, today, and forever.

While writing this book, I went through a difficult change. I gave up my job as a senior editor at Multnomah Publishers to pursue a full-time career in writing—a big step of faith for me. But God was leading and I followed.

It's been six months now, and I have no regrets. Writing at home has allowed me more time to spend with my family (I've even gotten a dog—a chocolate lab named Bailey) and pursue other interests. I work in my garden and tend my pond; I have romantic dates with my hubby; I walk my dog; and I'm getting better acquainted with my nearly grown sons.

I've also recently learned that three of my books are up for awards, and that's been a huge encouragement to me. My hope is to become a better writer and to continue to create stories and characters that touch people's lives. My prayer is that God will use me as his pen.

I've received many beautiful letters from readers and am trying to maintain a mailing list for newsletters. If I have somehow missed you, please try again; you have no idea how uplifting it is to hear readers' responses.

God's best to you!

Melody Carlson

You may write to Melody Carlson
c/o Palisades
P.O. Box 1720
Sisters, Oregon 97759

THE PALISADES LINE

Dalton's Dilemma, Lynn Bulock
ISBN 1-57673-238-X
Lacey Robbins, single mother of her sister's four children, is seeking adventure. But she never expected to find it by running into—literally!—handsome Jack Dalton at the roller rink. And she never expected the attraction between them to change her life forever....

Heartland Skies, Melody Carlson
ISBN 1-57673-264-9
Jayne Morgan moves to the small town of Paradise with the prospect of marriage, a new job, and plenty of horses to ride. But when her fiancé dumps her, she's left with loose ends. Then she wins a horse in a raffle, and the handsome rancher who boards her horse makes things look decidedly better.

Shades of Light, Melody Carlson
ISBN 1-57673-283-5
When widow Gwen Sullivan's daughter leaves for college, she discovers she can't bear her empty nest and takes a job at an interior decorating firm. But tedious work and a fussy boss leave her wondering if she's made the right move. Then Oliver Black, a prominent businessman, solicits her services and changes her mind....

Memories, Peggy Darty
ISBN 1-57673-171-5
In this sequel to *Promises,* Elizabeth Calloway is left with amnesia after witnessing a hit-and-run accident. Her husband, Michael, takes her on a vacation to Cancún so that she can relax and recover her memory. What they don't realize is that a killer is following them, hoping to wipe out Elizabeth's memory permanently....

Spirits, Peggy Darty (October 1998)
ISBN 1-57673-304-1
Picking up where *Memories* left off, the Calloways take a vacation to Angel Valley to find a missing woman. They enlist the help of a local writer who is an expert in Smoky Mountain legend and uncover a strange web of folklore and spirits.

Remembering the Roses, Marion Duckworth
ISBN 1-57673-236-3
Sammie Sternberg is trying to escape her memories of the man who betrayed her and ends up in a small town on the Olympic Peninsula in Washington. There she opens her dream business—an antique shop in an old Victorian—and meets a reclusive watercolor artist who helps to heal her broken heart.

Waterfalls, Robin Jones Gunn
ISBN 1-57673-221-5
In a visit to Glenbrooke, Oregon, Meredith Graham meets movie star Jacob Wilde and is sure he's the one. But when Meri puts her foot in her mouth, things fall apart. Is isn't until the two of them get thrown together working on a book-and-movie project that Jacob realizes his true feelings, and this time he's the one who's starstruck.

China Doll, Barbara Jean Hicks
ISBN 1-57673-262-2
Bronson Bailey is having a mid-life crisis: after years of globe-trotting in his journalism career, he's feeling restless. Georgine Nichols has also reached a turning point: after years of longing for a child, she's decided to adopt. The problem is, now she's fallen in love with Bronson, and he doesn't want a child.

Angel in the Senate, Kristen Johnson Ingram
ISBN 1-57673-263-0
Newly elected senator Megan Likely heads to Washington with high hopes for making a difference in government. But accusations of election fraud, two shocking murders, and threats on her life make the Senate take a back seat. She needs to find answers, but she's not sure who she can trust anymore.

Irish Rogue, Annie Jones
ISBN 1-57673-189-8
Michael Shaughnessy has paid the price for stealing a pot of gold, and now he's ready to make amends to the people he's hurt. Fiona O'Dea is number one on his list. The problem is, Fiona doesn't want to let Michael near enough to hurt her again. But before she knows it, he's taken his Irish charm and worked his way back into her life...and her heart.

Beloved, Deb Kastner
ISBN 1-57673-331-9
Wanted: A part-time pastor with a full-time heart for a wedding ministry. When wedding coordinator Kate Logan places the ad for a pastor, she doesn't expect a man like Todd Jensen to apply. But she quickly learns that he's perfect for the job—and perfect for her heart.

On Assignment, Marilyn Kok
ISBN 1-57673-279-7
When photographer Tessa Brooks arrives in Singapore for an assignment, she's both excited and nervous about seeing her ex-fiancé, banker Michael Lawton. Michael has mixed feelings, too: he knows he still loves Tessa, but will he ever convince her that they can get past the obstacle of their careers and make their relationship work?

Forgotten, Lorena McCourtney
ISBN 1-57673-222-3
A woman wakes up in an Oregon hospital with no memory of who she is. When she's identified as Kat Cavanaugh, she returns to her home in California. As Kat struggles to recover her memory, she meets a fiancé she doesn't trust and an attractive neighbor who can't believe how she's changed. She begins to wonder if she's really Kat Cavanaugh, but if she isn't, what happened to the real Kat?

Canyon, Lorena McCourtney (September 1998)
ISBN 1-57673-287-8
Kit Holloway and Tyler McCord are wildly in love, planning their wedding, and looking forward to a summer of whitewater rafting through the Grand Canyon. Then the actions of two people they love rip apart their relationship. Can their love survive, or will their differences prove to be too much?

Rustlers, Karen Rispin (September 1998)
ISBN 1-57673-292-4
Amber Lacey is on the run—from her home, from her career, and from God. She ends up working on a ranch in western

Alberta and trying to keep the secrets of her past from the man she's falling in love with. But then sinister dealings on the ranch force Amber to confront the mistakes she's made—and turn back to the God who never gave up on her.

The Key, Gayle Roper
ISBN 1-57673-223-1
On Kristie Matthews's first day living on an Amish farm, she gets bitten by a dog and is rushed to the emergency room by a handsome stranger. In the ER, an elderly man in the throes of a heart attack hands her a key and tells her to keep it safe. Suddenly odd accidents begin to happen to her, but no one's giving her any answers.

The Document, Gayle Roper (October 1998)
ISBN 1-57673-295-9
While Cara Bentley is sorting through things after the death of her grandfather, she stumbles upon evidence that he was adopted. Determined to find her roots, she heads to Lancaster County and settles in at an Amish farm. She wants to find out who she is, but she can't help wondering: if it weren't for the money in John Bentley's will, would anyone else care about her identity?

ANTHOLOGIES

Fools for Love, Ball, Brooks, Jones
ISBN 1-57673-235-5
By Karen Ball: Kitty starts pet-sitting, but when her clients turn out to be more than she can handle, she enlists help from a handsome handyman.

By Jennifer Brooks: Caleb Murphy tries to acquire a book collection from a widow, but she has one condition: he must marry her granddaughter first.

By Annie Jones: A college professor who has been burned by love vows not to be fooled twice, until her ex-fiancé shows up and ruins her plans!

Heart's Delight, Ball, Hicks, Noble
ISBN 1-57673-220-7
By Karen Ball: Corie receives a Valentine's Day date from her sisters and thinks she's finally found the one…until she learns she went out with the wrong man.

By Barbara Jean Hicks: Carina and Reid are determined to break up their parents' romance, but when it looks like things are working, they have a change of heart.

By Diane Noble: Two elderly bird-watchers set aside their differences to try to save a park from disaster, but learn they've bitten off more than they can chew.

Be sure to look for any of the 1997 titles you may have missed:

Surrender, Lynn Bulock (ISBN 1-57673-104-9)
Single mom Cassie Neel accepts a blind date from her children for her birthday.

Wise Man's House, Melody Carlson (ISBN 1-57673-070-0)
A young widow buys her childhood dream house, and a mysterious stranger moves into her caretaker's cottage.

Moonglow, Peggy Darty (ISBN 1-57673-112-X)
Tracy Kosell comes back to Moonglow, Georgia, and investigates a case with a former schoolmate, who's now a detective.

Promises, Peggy Darty (ISBN 1-57673-149-9)
A Christian psychologist asks her detective husband to help her find a dangerous woman.

Texas Tender, Sharon Gillenwater (ISBN 1-57673-111-1)
Shelby Nolan inherits a watermelon farm and asks the sheriff for help when two elderly men begin digging holes in her fields.

Clouds, Robin Jones Gunn (ISBN 1-57673-113-8)
Flight attendant Shelly Graham runs into her old boyfriend, Jonathan Renfield, and learns he's engaged.

Sunsets, Robin Jones Gunn (ISBN 1-57673-103-0)
Alissa Benson has a run-in at work with Brad Phillips, and is more than a little upset when she finds out he's her neighbor!

Snow Swan, Barbara Jean Hicks (ISBN 1-57673-107-3)
Toni, an unwed mother and a recovering alcoholic, falls in love for the first time. But if Clark finds out the truth about her past, will he still love her?

Irish Eyes, Annie Jones (ISBN 1-57673-108-1)
Julia Reed gets drawn into a crime involving a pot of gold and has her life turned upside-down by Interpol agent Cameron O'Dea.

Father by Faith, Annie Jones (ISBN 1-57673-117-0)
Nina Jackson buys a dude ranch and hires cowboy Clint Cooper as her foreman, but her son, Alex, thinks Clint is his new daddy!

Stardust, Shari MacDonald (ISBN 1-57673-109-X)
Gillian Spencer gets her dream assignment but is shocked to learn she must work with Maxwell Bishop, who once broke her heart.

Kingdom Come, Amanda MacLean (ISBN 1-57673-120-0)
Ivy Rose Clayborne, M.D., pairs up with the grandson of the coal baron to fight the mining company that is ravaging her town.

Dear Silver, Lorena McCourtney (ISBN 1-57673-110-3)
When Silver Sinclair receives a letter from Chris Bentley ending their relationship, she's shocked, since she's never met the man!

Enough! Gayle Roper (ISBN 1-57673-185-5)
When Molly Gregory gets fed up with her three teenaged children, she announces that she's going on strike.

A Mother's Love, Bergren, Colson, MacLean (ISBN 1-57673-106-5)
Three heartwarming stories share the joy of a mother's love.

Silver Bells, Bergren, Krause, MacDonald (ISBN 1-57673-119-7)
Three novellas focus on romance during Christmastime.

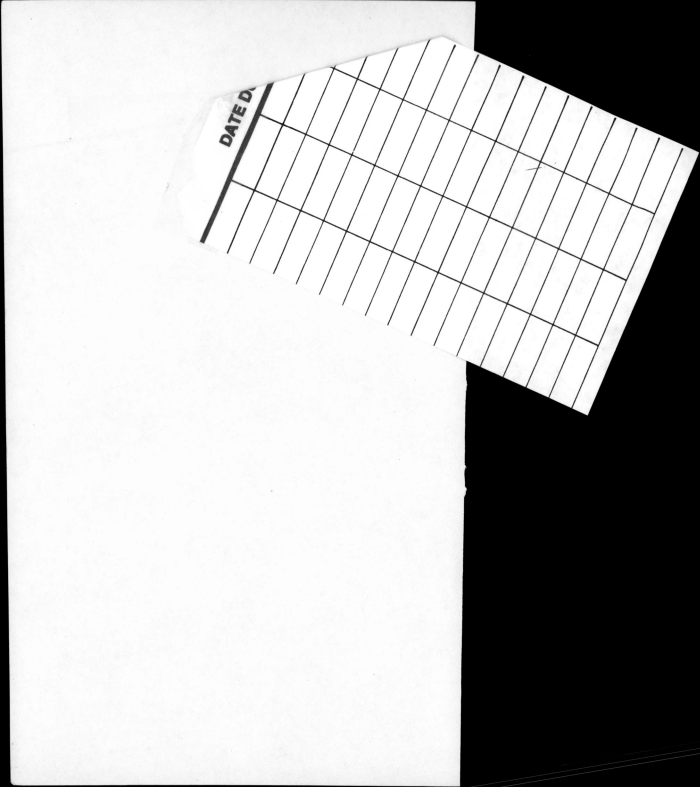

DATE D